THE HOODOO

THE GREAT BLACK BOOK OF GENERATIONS

Arthur Rickydoc Flowers

Rootwork Press

Rootwork Press

Copyright © 2020 by Arthur Flowers

ISBN: 978-1-734101911

All rights reserved, including the right to reproduce this book or portions thereof in any form whatsoever. For information address info@rootworkpress.org.

Cover design by David Wojciechowski / davidwojo.com

Interior layout by Arthur Flowers and David Wojciechowski

Cover Art *Long Distance Runner* by Tom Feelings

Table of Contents

1ˢᵀ Movement: INITIATION 1

    1:1: hoodoo consciousness 2

    1:2: hoodoo survival 5

    1:3: hoodoo tribulation 8

    1:4: hoodoo will 11

    1:5: hoodoo law 13

    1:6: hoodoo character: 16

    1:7: hoodoo spiritwork 18

2ᴺᴰ MOVEMENT: STRUGGLE 21

    2:8: hoodoo struggle 21

    2:9: hoodoo fortitude 23

    2:10: hoodoo blues 26

    2:11: hoodoo agency 28

    2:12: hoodoo fortune 31

    2:13: hoodooing transgression 35

    2:14: hoodoo redemption 37

3ᴿᴰ MOVEMENT: LIFEWORKS 41

    3:15: hoodoo youth 41

    3:16: hoodoo family 43

    3:17: hoodoo knowledge 46

    3:18: hoodoo work 49

    3:19: hoodoo love 51

    3:20: hoodoo finance 55

    3:21: hoodoo maturity 58

4ᵀᴴ MOVEMENT: THE CHANGES 61

    4:22: hoodoo eldership 61
    4:23: hoodoo deathbed blues... 63
    4:24: hoodoo growthing... 66
    4:25: hoodoo mojo 68
    4:26: hoodoo time 71
    4:27: hoodoo journeys.. 74

5TH MOVEMENT: SERVICE 79

    5:29: hoodoo stewardship 79
    5:30: hoodoo community 82
    5:31: hoodoo organizing... 84
    5:32: hoodoo guidance:... 88
    5:33: hoodoo strategy.. 91
    5:34: hoodoo leadership... 93
    5:35: hoodoo governance... 95

6TH MOVEMENT: EMPOWERMENT 99

    6:36: hoodoo power 99
    6:37: hoodoo gatherings..101
    6:38: hoodoo sciTech 104
    6:39: hoodoo war 106
    6:40: hoodoo rootwork 108
    6:41: hoodoo longgame..111
    6:42: hoodoo nobility 114

7TH MOVEMENT: DESTINYWORK...................................117

    7:43: hoodoo wordcraft 117
    7:44: hoodoo mythwork 119
    7:45: the hoodoo way...123

7:46: hoodoo magic 126
7:47: hoodoo conjuration 129
7:48: hoodoo prophecy 131
7:49: hoodoo destinywork 135

8TH MOVEMENT: ILLUMINATION 140

8:50: hoodoo wisdom 140
8:51: hoodoo compassion 142
8:52: hoodoo meditation 144
8:53: hoodoo illumination 148
8:54: hoodoo cleansing 151
8:55: hoodoo crossroads 154
8:56: hoodoo faith 156

9TH MOVEMENT: IRIE GRACE 160

9:57: hoodoo serenity 160
9:58: hoodoo mastery 162
9:59: hoodoo transcendent 164
9:60: hoodoo blessings 167
9:61: hoodoo grace 169
9:62: hoodoo Fa 171
9:63: hoodoo godwork 173

I am Flowers of the Delta Clan Flowers and the Line of O Killens. I offer this Work in the name of Babajohn Killens. The Great Griot Master of Brooklyn. He who taught me to see. A toolbox. An armory. A hoodoo manual. This is the Text. This is the Way.

thats what love, cooperation and unity are in a society, a comforter, Im a comforter for my people, so I have great dominion and power, glory and authority, but I use my discretion and my people love I, because I heal their afflictions, ras hui-I

The Hoodoo Book of Flowers

1ST Movement: INITIATION
help me god, open mine eyes that I might see
open my heart that I might be

1:1: hoodoo consciousness
lor*d legba, open this gate, in the name*
of the conqueror let this work be done

1:1:1: welcome o traveler, let us begin with I am, consciousness - *know thyself* - the greatest struggle, the greatest power - *who am I? why am I here? what is the point?* - a pilgrim once come upon the babajohn and said *I seek the babajohn*, the babajohn replied, *so do I,*

1:1:2: consciousness must be selfawareness, the ability to step back and monitor yourself, to be capable of encompassing the moment from a higher and more dispassionate plane, able to watch yourself thinking / emoting / being / monitoring the forces shaping you, within and without - *know thyself* was the 1st maxim of the delphic oracle,

1:1:3: on a cosmic scale human life is the barest blink, the minute you born the clock is ticking and you falling behind, become conscious quick as you can, choose your path, articulate a contribution to the enhancement of the human condition, devote your life to it and the care of loved ones, die easy, satisfied - *I done good, short time I was here, I done good,*

1:1:4: the soul can only be consciousness, what else can it be, weak at birth it becomes stronger as we become more selfaware, selfguided, its evolution the measure of your growth, it is consciousness that allows you to shape your life, only then can you master your own destiny instead of being tossed about by the winds of circumstance, subject to the whims of others - but if the soul is consciousness, what then the immensity of the supraconsciousness that links us to the universal divinity / the great mojo / the ineffable touch of eternity,

1:1:5: initiation of the soul is not a given, we, all of us, start life ignorant & asleep, as we mature our understanding of real increases and we conduct ourselves accordingly, our lives become more harmonious, we are initiated - the spiritual life doesnt just happen, it is an active choice, nurturance of the soul is the goal of this Work - *open your eyes, young conjure* - a step every soul must take, look deep and tell me, what do you see, what is consciousness & who knows when the only thing certain is we are surely blind & wisdom must be won again and again and again,

1:1:6: in the beginning was the mojo, then bang there was the great mojo and the cosmos begin to manifest entity / eternity, desperately seeking Fa and spewing seeds of stellar dust that become one big great thing - galaxies / suns / planets / peoples / we is the universe, the universe is us - *and the great mojo called it good* - then, in the fullness of time, here come humanity, leap frogging from the primal muck to stand upright, tools in hand, eyes on the stars, ever questing to be greater than we are,

1:1:7: for this testimony let us call on mother lucy, the monkey doctor, first of the monkey people to stand on two feet - I believe, she told them, if we stand on our hind legs that our tribe and all our generations will flourish, I believe we can be more than we are, like this, she say, and then she stand, and o my god, she say, if only you could see what I see, from here I can see the stars, from here I can see forever - at which point the monkey folk scoff, why on earth, they say, would we want to do that, what can we possibly do on 2 feet that we cannot do better on 4, why, o fool of a dreamer, would the great monkey god give us 4 feet if not to use them - but mambo lucy, she persist, listen, she exhort, many years I have birthed, taught and tended you, all for this one time I must be heard, Fa has come to us, a journey like nothing this world has seen, the long march of the firstborn has begun, and there, she point at the stars in the sky, is where it will end, come, let us begin,

1:1:8: ok, too much too soon maybe, went cosmological on you, safer perhaps to begin with legba, lord of the crossroads & keeper of the gates, opener of doors between this world and de spirit world, messenger of de gods and de random factors, he who must be petitioned at the beginning of any spiritwork - legba flourished in the americas, in dahomey he is an outlaw, a trickster, a profane flouter of tradition, in dahomey he lacks moral fiber and makes his own rules, in dahomey he is mawu-lisa's linquist, custodian of the crossroads and divine writ - when the realms of human custodianship were divided amongst the loa, legba, the youngest loa, found himself with nothing to do, and so he was given the space between realms, made keeper of the gates, now whenever you attempt spiritwork you must 1st ask legba to open the gate, for it is in the beginning of things that paths are laid, destinies shaped - most folk go through life asleep, zombies walking, but this moment is a conscious one, another sleeper has awakened, a better you been born,

1:1:9: it is altogether possible to go through life without a shred of consciousness, to never truly question yourself, to live an unexamined life – its possible but I wouldnt personally advise autozombification and there is no rush, young spiritdoctor, quite like awakening sleepers, one of the 3 pillars of hoodoo - *awaken the sleeper, protect the weak, guide the strong* – manner of speaking we all sleepers, nobody more than I.

*Fa is upon you, o traveler, embrace it
with a hoodoo passion for life,*

this is the text
this is the way

demoja

1:2: hoodoo survival
*I call on he who thought the world
& then it was so, lord ptah creator*

1:2:1: I survive, I endure, I am, listen o traveler, this one thing you must do, the fundamental task of all life is to survive, grindhouse, all day every day, aint no standing still, if you aint gaining ground you falling behind - *every breath drawn is an act of survival* - 1st you must secure the basics, food, shelter, security, companionship, these things, once the basics are secured we indulge the higher nature, significance, honor, dignity, meaning, the high road,

1:2:2: then there is finessing the survival moment, a survival moment is always a crossroads, out of nowhere everything is suddenly at stake, from nowhere its do or die, the immediate response to a survival moment is panic and loss of control, yet it is precisely in the critical moment that the hoodoo practitioner is able to repress panic and become ruthlessly logical, a walking meditation trained to the hoodoo blink,

1:2:3: sometime survival (god help us) is beyond personal, sometimes its survival of the family / unit / community / tribe / humanity / all things, sometimes the stakes are bigger than you and honor your only call, *the only sacrifice I will accept is your own,*

1:2:4: in any given era the weight of history lies upon some peoples, in the dawn of history africa of the nile was in the game, but what was once strong is now weak, the 1st have become the last, the race worn out and in decline, or can redemption be found, greater purpose, perhaps, in de geas of rickydoc,

1:2:5: cultural survival in a globalized world will be determined by which cultures thrive and contribute vs which ones wither and die, I would the hoodoo way be a better way, one folk aspire to, an african american way, the magical negro wrote large, I too have been to the mountaintop, I too have seen the promiseland & this what I see - a *culture healthy, wealthy and wise, respected throughout the cosmos, guide and guardian of humanitys eternal quest to evolve, to be greater than we are,*

1:2:6: also I see human survival require getting off the planet, extinction events happen, its not if, its when, global warming, rogue meteors, nuclear winters, whatever, one planet is not enough to insure survival of the species, got to spread out, increase the odds, I would you be a star faring peoples, adept at bringing down the mothership, witness ***freedom means*** by the dells: *we're children of the sun / and we're heading home again / theres a long journey ahead, we might as well begin / our true selves are somewhere out beyond the stars / we got to try uniting / got to make a whole new scene / maybe then we will understand, what freedom means. . .*

1:2:7: if we were to wipe ourselves out or fall prey to a random asteroid, likely the immensity of the universe would not even notice our passing, but if we do survive / get off the planet / become a starfaring peoples / transhumanization might finesse end of time / universe theories, *the big brakes / crunches / freezes / lurches / rips / singularities / whimpers / whatever* - same way we have evolved through apes and proto-humans this is not the final stage, future folk will consider us crudely formed savages, some will insist that they couldnt possibly be related to us,

1:2:8: but what, you ask, of megadeath, death not of your choosing, earthquakes, volcanos, twisters, floods & war, death without regard for worth or station, it appears the universe is no respecter of worth, when the planet shifts in search of its own equanimity folk suffer, when solar systems shrug planets die, waste neither time nor heart with why me lord, reach for a hoodoo survival mode and sing your very best deathbed blues - if you do survive, position yourself for the comeback, rebuild better, stronger - *no blame,*

1:2:9: survival can never be allowed to degrade us, it is precisely in the throes of survival that honor is most critical, a good foundation blesses all that comes after and survival at all costs is not survival, the demands of survival must always ennoble and not demean us, witness mlkings admonition that struggle must always call us to our very best - *in the process of gaining our rightful place, we must not be guilty of wrongful deeds. let us not seek to satisfy our thirst for freedom by drinking from the cup of bitterness and hatred. we must forever conduct our struggle on the high plane of dignity and discipline,*

The Hoodoo Book of Flowers

I believe humanity will meet every challenge, I have to believe this or I would despair - I believe come the hammer, come the vision, I believe there is always a way, I believe in you,

demoja

1:3: hoodoo tribulation
apedemak rest on jebal barkals seat,
there is no trouble I cannot beat,
no burden I cannot bear,

1:3:1: unto each life there must be trouble, unto each measure trial and tribulation, no such thing as a life without trouble, if there was it wouldnt be of any use to you, it is through tribulation that we grow strong, it is through tribulation that the outdated is abandoned, it is only stripped of the inessential that you appreciate whats essential / meaningful, it is through tribulation that the soul is seasoned,

1:3:2: I recall when folk come to the babajohn complaining about their troubles, so the babajohn suggest they put their troubles in bags we will hang from the great bottletree, then you can each choose a set of troubles other than your own - well, as you can imagine, the community thought this was an excellent idea so everybody hung their troubles on the great bottletree and then they all went around inspecting the various sacks of woe, trying on other folks troubles until in the final round they had each chose their own - *since it appear everybody got trouble might as well keep the trouble you know,*

1:3:3: the babajohn asked them, do you really want knowledge without difficulty, attainment without effort, progress without sacrifice, the ocean without the roar of its mighty waters - yes, yes, of course, the people replied, thats exactly what we want, well, say the babajohn, if you find it let me know, Id like to get some, too,

1:3:4: trouble is finessed through reflection and positioning yourself for the comeback, land on higherground and you have finessed it, transformed trouble into power, tribulation into strength - trouble aint nothing but a testing, the challenge no more than preparation for the next task at hand,

1:3:5: trouble come to ancient egypt in waves - hyskos / assyrians / romans / greeks / arabs / black egypt retreating, step by step, inch by inch, until assyrians under usertesen iii had the nerve to raise a granite stele at semnah said - *no black man whatsoever shall be permitted to pass this place* - but the palermo stone records victories of africans from the capitals of nekheb, thebes and napata, the stele of una reports that armies of blacks from yam, wawat, mazoi, kau and temeh sprang fullgrown out of the desert and galactic nubia was born in the call of apedemak, wargod of de nubians, and amesami, patron of de kandakes, Im told it is the elders of kush called forth them what reside on jebal barkals peak, sacred mountain of nubia, them what make do in the hearts of us all - *apedemak give me guidance, support me, revitalize me, guide me to reverent satisfaction, that I may go forth, that the moon arise, that warriors of nubia awake,*

1:3:6: back in the day brer alligator had that smooth pretty skin made him feel superior to otherfolk, one day he dis brer rabbit and it really dont do to dis da rabbit, so the next day here come brer rabbit looking at he watch and talking about Im late,

Im late, Im really, really late, now everybody know you dont ask no rabbit what he late for less you ready for the looking glass but brer alligator a curious creature, he say where to, brer rabbit, and the rabbit say Im going to meet trouble, surely you know trouble, big man in these parts, own all the land, brer alligator say sound like somebody I need to know, mind if I tag along, the rabbit say sure, bring the family - so he take the alligator family to that big field down by the riverside and say yall wait right here, Ima go get trouble, then he go to the other side of the field and he start a great big fire, the alligator family see the flames but all that pretty red, yellow and orange packaging dazzle them, and they thinking my, my, dont trouble look fine, so they standing there waiting on trouble, and by and by that fire got them surrounded and they feel the heat of the flame, and they allow its time to move, and they are right next to the water - *right next to the water* - but to get to the water - *to get to the water* - they must go through the fire - *go through the fire* - so the alligator family they scoot through the fire and into the water, and they get away – *they get away* - but they get all scorched up and thats why, to this day, when you see brer alligator he gon have a wrinkled up skin, and when you see sister alligator, she aint gon be too far from the water - *aint gon be too far from the water* - and if you speak to any of the little alligator chillen for more than a minute or two, they will tell you - *dont go looking for trouble, not unless trouble come looking for you,*

1:3:7: *now into each life there must be trouble,* and into each life just a little bit of rain, otherwise dont nothing grow, but god dont give you no burden you cant carry, and it is only through adversity that you will ever know your true strength - so when the hard times come I want you to hold on, you must be strong, you fight the battles, friend, nobody else could win, next time you find yourself in trouble, I want you to remember what the old blues doctor said,

*every goodbye it aint gone, cause you sick dont mean
you dead, trouble dont last, trouble dont last always*

demoja demoja demoja
trouble dont last always

1:4: hoodoo will
*kandakes do not retreat and neither do I,
I will not be defeated, I will not be denied*

1:4:1: to will, to do, to be able, doing what you know you need to do when you know you need to do it, any level of achievement requires the application of the disciplined will, without the severe discipline of the great player you not in the game, how can you be free if you cannot command yourself with the ruthless selfdiscipline of those who would master their own destiny / Fa,

1:4:2: the key to discipline is consistency, if its not consistent its not discipline, set up a regular time and place, take care of your business, come back tomorrow and do it again, make discipline a habit / religion / lifelong struggle / way of life / every move pregnant with point and purpose, do not drift, plan your life and every step in it, the earlier the better, awaken o sleeper, arise,

1:4:3: the hoodoo way accepts responsibility for whatever befall you, whatever it was it got through your game - *my bad,* *ima do better* - pride yourself on the quality of your moves, ongoing adjustments to life / terrain, planned envelopments so precisely sequenced, so exquisitely calibrated even stillness is action, the fruit of timing, positioning & the decisive moment, position yourself to live out your greatest dreams, horse of the kandakes, warrior queens who stopped rome at the gates of africa,

1:4:4: it is your duty, your responsibility to yourself, to be greater than you are, it is your duty, your responsibility to others, that ensures the survival of us all - it is a willingness to sacrifice that buttress every great deed, doing what must be done simply because it must, responsibility, duty, these measures of maturity and functions of nobility - acts of will must serve the common good, do what you will is a soulless principle, if all you do is for yourself, young conjure, you little better than a beast, the hoodoo will must always be leavened with the compassion of o killens,

1:4:5: of the 7 princesses in this text, ombure the crocodile god had already eaten 6, only then were the villagers allowed food of their own, but when soueinas time came she convinced her royal father to abdicate in her name - y*ou might sacrifice a princess*, soueina told her people, *but you will not sacrifice a queen, tell ombure its war,*

1:4:6: without moderation your strengths become your weaknesses, too much strength wont bend, unbending power will consume itself,

1:4:7: once you conscious of yourself as selfguided and ultimately malleable you shape life to your liking, you make a plan, you gain the necessary skills, you position yourself, you assume you can do anything anybody else has done and always be willing to do a little more than anybody else would - *you are the ascensionist, are you not, what others dream you do,*

demoja

1:5: hoodoo law
dearest maat, attune me to thy universe,

1:5:1: the individual will, the drive to be, hammers itself against the iron constraints of reality and the immutable laws of nature. to live a life of grace and successful adaptation to your environment is to live in accordance with the natural laws, an ongoing process of understanding and harmonization in which every thought / word / act / deed takes you closer to, or further away, from godhead,

1:5:2: some natural laws are as evident as food, shelter and security, some are more esoteric but none the less important to a life of grace, cooperation is a natural law that ensures survival of the species, and I suspect your actions do affect the state of your immortal soul, and likely it is better to give than to receive, spiritually speaking - principles like do unto others, karma, and the law of return are based on the natural law that you become what you into, if you thinking *hurt somebody* the soul crippled is your own,

1:5:3: in an orderly society law must be mutually respected, justice must be perceived as fair and impartial, if you would your citizens not be subject to the whims of the powerful protection of the powerless must be institutionalized, I recall the time brer fox got his hands on sister goose though means dark and unlawful, o I got you now, sister goose, he say, Ima kill you, Ima eat you, then Ima pick your bones, o no, say sister goose, I got rights and according to my rights this catch is unlawful, so sister goose take brother fox to court, but when she walk in the door she note that the judge is a fox, the jury is foxes, the sheriff and the bailiff both is foxes, so they go ahead and they try her, they execute and they eat her, and then they pick her bones,

1:5:4. *there is always a cost incurred in breaking a law,* human or natural, always, make sure its worth it, abolition, a civil rights movement, destinywork, goals of this sort show a respect for law that goes beyond the letter, you got to know when to break it, finesse it, demand it, manipulate it - when mulatresse solitude was captured after a rebellion on guadeloupe the law was that a pregnant woman could not be executed, she petitioned to deliver her own replacement in the struggle, was hung the day after but her line lives on,

1:5:5: *among the highest levels of grace* is to give justice without expecting justice in return, laws are written to serve society and must evolve as we do, laws must always be bathed in justice, those who uphold the law must always be careful of crippling souldeath, just cause you wallowing in the mud dont mean you got to get dirty,

1:5:6: *once upon a time on the edge of night and day*, brer rabbit hear a mournful howl, *whoop whoop whooooo,* who there, ask brer rabbit, he hold up the lantern he carrying when he hear a voice sad as it can be asking is that you, brer rabbit, this brer wolf, need some help here, at which point brer rabbit peer over the edge of the road and there brer wolf is under a rock and sorely aggrieved, dont know that helping you is to my advantage, say brer rabbit, you been mighty keen on having me and mine for dinner, but brer wolf say please, brer rabbit, this one time and I will never bother you and yours no more - now brer rabbit a good hearted creature mostly, so he scoot over and pull brer wolf free and right away brer wolf scoop him up and say, I got you now, but you promised say brer rabbit, I wont trust you ever again, and brer wolf say you wont nothing ever again but just then judge tortoise come ambling through, having just now left court she still in her robes and brer rabbit petition her for a reading, your opinion on this matter, your honor, please, brer rabbit say he should not be penalized for a moment of fellowship and brer wolf say I caught him fair and square, the judge say this is a very tough case, perhaps if I could see the original situation, whereupon they convince brer wolf to get back under the rock, then they stand there for some time discussing the particulars whilst brer wolf wonder if yall could perhaps hurry the proceedings along, this rock mighty heavy, finally da judge clear her throat and say I have made my decision, you guilty, brer rabbit, of terminal foolishness, you guilty, brer rabbit, of not leaving well enough alone, and on that note she up and take her leave, but when brer rabbit prepare to hop off, brer wolf say what about me, the rabbit say fool me once shame on you, fool me twice shame on me, and he hop on off too, leaving brer wolf crying out whenever he see a full moon and think its brer rabbit with his lantern, *whoop whoop whoooooo, whoop whoop whoooooo,*

1:5:7: understand the universal laws, o traveler, and you will have received a blessing of great import, maat, the egyptian god of justice, weighs each soul against a feather, if you are blameless, your sins lighter than the feather, you are allowed to pass, if not you are consumed, egypts focus on justice, on law and regulation came out of her need to regulate the life giving rhythms of the nile, conduct yourself in accordance to the natural laws and the universe will bless you and yours, bless everything you do,

as will rickydoc, all my love, all my
blessings, demoja demoja demoja
whoop whoop whooooooooooooooo

1:6: hoodoo character:
my lady douthet, come, show me the way

1:6:1: the hoodoo way is grounded in the pursuit of character, the hoodoo path seeks not altered states but illuminated traits of character and the daily refinement thereof, forging a good soul, a citizen of the world, an example of values you consider essential in the world you want to live in, forging yourself into what the iching calls a *superior personality* is the goal of all the great paths,

1:6:2: the traits of good character have been consistent long as folk been keeping records, the great ways pretty much all ask for the same thing, that you treat others as you would be treated, that you carry yourself at all times with honor / dignity / gravitas, that you value courage / perseverance / integrity / compassion / wisdom / fairness, these things, a sense of responsibility for self & others, a certain generosity of spirit, the same things parents have tried to pass on generation after generation,

1:6:3: hoodoo theology you got two souls, the home soul and the traveling soul, the traveling spirit the one that travel about in dreams, visions, astral projections and the like, the home soul is your personal slice of the great mojo - *I. Am. Master. Here.* - it is the home soul that is responsible for your integrity, the one keep a steady course in the maelstrom of forces pulling at you, the one what keep you whole and healthy, it is a soulshield while the traveling spirit is an aggressor, manifesting itself into the world, the point of the spear, it is the traveling spirit go ancestral when the home soul returns to the source,

1:6:4: character is how you present yourself to the world, adorn yourself not in jewels but hoodoo jewelry - honor / dignity / gravitas / these things - treasure your reputation, character is not something you find along the way, you forge it, brick by brick, stone by stone, a spiritual work of art, and always best to remember, one lie spoils a dozen truths, one venal act a lifetime of grace,

1:6:5: avoid any behavior that lacks honor, anything that does not reek of nobility and grace, when soul fevers like anger / envy / pettiness of any sort come down on you just observe them, do not fight them, do not attach emotional value, just assess & finesse, if anything amused, avoid anything of which I would not approve, anything other than the good and great soul I would you be,

1:6:6: conduct yourself as you aspire to be and you are, this is the essence of conjuration, this is the essence of character - *always strive to be the greater you, to be greater than you are, evolve* - every decision is a crossroads from which we will either evolve or devolve,

1:6:7: and please do not come crying to me about the conditions of your birth, oppression does not define you, adversity is just another opportunity to extract good character traits from the crucible of struggle, embrace the hammer, your goal during your brief sojourn on the planet is to forge a good if not great soul, which can be manifested only through character,

The Hoodoo Book of Flowers

*from thoughts actions, from actions habits,
from habits character, character destiny,*

get your mojo on

demoja

1:7: hoodoo spiritwork
*mama dreamsoul, soul dreaming
creatrix, let this dream be*

1:7:1: *every soul is on a journey,* a quest to be, a search for meaning and fulfillment, a quest for your place in the universe, an effort to make your time on the planet significant through your soulwork, the soul is the only thing thats real / permanent / essential / eternal / your personal slice of the great mojo, everything else is transient adornment,

1:7:2: *you do not possess a spiritual life merely by existing,* spiritlife it is a conscious choice, humans are born amoral, deep in the physical / animal nature, driven by impulse and desire, the soul is made whole by socialization, by training, by the relentless pursuit of the spiritual, by avoiding the lowroad, avoiding anything that degrades you - communion with the divine is your birthright, *listen to the voice of Fa*, the one that always knows the way, everything in the universe speaks to those who listen, those who follow the pilgrims path,

1:7:3: *blues gospel according to ray charles:* *Ive fooled around the way blacks have been doing for years, playing the blues to*

different rhythms, that style requires pure heart singing, later on they would call it soul music,

1:7:4: everything benefits from the conscious life, most folk live in the material world with just an occasional touch of the spirit, the conjuror is a two headed individual with one face in the material and the other in the spiritual, able upon the blink of the hoodoo eye to segue into a spiritual plane, to see through illusion, deal with folk spirit to spirit, a deeper plane of engagement,

1:7:5: the bonded soul actively searches out crossroads moments through which it surmounts the constraints of the material world, a personal journey tailored to your Fa / destiny - at birth we are given a soul, a fertile blend of the personal, the collective, and divinity, we are expected in our lifetime to shape raw soul into a spiritual work of art - according to the legbara the soul is weak at birth, increasing in strength as it ages until at death it joins the ancestral ranks, according to the legbara a life rich in grace forges a soul worthy of ancestral ground, according to the legbara there is a little mojo in every soul,

1:7:6: when the fula armies of seku amadu lobbo bari came to conquer the bambara the warrior fale tankara engaged amadu in a battle of champions, but tankaras bullets bounced off amadus many talismans and amadus sword would not bite until amadu hit fale tankara with the horsewhisk of mohammed and tankaras talismans fell to the ground, impressed with his bravery amadu offered to spare him if fale tankara would give his soul to the crescent, fale tankara refused and fale tankara died, fale tankara lives forever in de geas of rickydoc,

1:7:7: the path of the spirit is one of eternal vigilance, it is a very crooked way, full of illusion - questions for which there are no answers I choose to believe what makes me stronger in the world, I choose to believe the more you live a life of the spirit the more likely your spirit will survive the death of the body, I believe the goal of all things hoodoo is an all encompassing generosity of spirit that blesses everything it touches, that enabalates divinity,

it is acts of grace that
renew the bonded soul

demoja

2ND MOVEMENT: STRUGGLE
give me strength, help me hold,

2:8: hoodoo struggle
come, come, alakoye, he who does the
hard things, come finesse this hammer

2:8:1: struggle, struggle, everyday everyway, struggle, waste neither time nor heart bemoaning your lot, everybody struggling, all day you struggle hard as anyone can, wake up the next morning got to do it again - *struggle or die are your options, nothing more, nothing less* - but is it not adversity that seasons the soul, take joy in the game, embrace it, reverses come when you not prepared, been caught unawares - good strategic posture should always be prepared for contingencies unforeseen, you reach too high, o traveler, not to fall now & then, make an art of dusting yourself off, thwarted by circumstance the superior personality remains true, hold on

2:8:2: sometime no matter how well you play you lose, sometime you just got to take the hammer, got hellhounds on your trail look like the creek didnt throw them and dear god you bout done but when hellhounds got the scent you just run shake the devil out your soul and outrun hot saliva scarring your neck but it really dont matter now cause you got your wind now and you flying cross dryground now and by god and all thats holy aint none of these fuckers gon outswim me,

2:8:3: some broken souls grow deep, they are transformed and empowered by suffering, they adjust, they finesse, they evolve while some folk their suffering just break them, suffering must be transformed into understanding through reflection and positioning yourself for a comeback, the key is to land in stronger position than whence you went down, use everything that happens to you as an invitation to growth, spiritual alchemists are always prepared to begin again,

2:8:4: gassire, one of the 7 sons of fasa and a warrior born, wanted his fathers shield but the diviners told him you will never get his shield, you will get his lute and wagadu will fall, you will not be king, you will be griot, at 1st dismissive of this curious fate it began to worry at him and so gassire had a lute made and was relieved when he could not make it sing, it has no soul, said the diviners, you must carry it on your back into the next battle, and so he did, and one by one, the 7 sons of gassire died in that battle, and one by one he carried them home on his back, and one by one, their blood soaked into the lute of gassire, and on the 7th day the lute began to sing, a tale of tragedy and elation and sacrifice, the ancient tale of wagadu, and gassire finally wept for his sons and the loss of wagadu but the rage that had consumed his soul was dissipated and his spirit was renewed in a vision of wagadu only he could see, and gassire sang again and again the tale of wagadus fall, of the 4 gates of wagadu that live forever in the songs of gassire de griot, for the heart sees what the eyes do not and wagadu lives again and again in the dreams of newborns, hear the clash of spears against the dreamshields of wagadu, listen to her songs, her tales, know her spirit and know when destroyed she returns in power, 4 times wagadou will fall, of vanity, dishonesty, greed, and discord, from vanity will come the griots song, from dishonesty riches, from greed a vision, from discord a new world - in each and every soul wagadu will be found,

2:8:5: the great encirclement crippled africa, arabs north and east, europeons west and south, and everywhere african against african, the strong became slavers, the weak became slaves,

The Hoodoo Book of Flowers

must have been an lack of historical clarity cause muhammed ali to name himself after one of the most prolific slavers / killers of blacks to ever depopulate the sudan - crescent and cross, east and west, must all be made to understand that they are guests in africa and not conquerors, swallow aggressors from the desert with strategic grace, be a better way, *I have been told that long as jebal barkal stands the nubians will not be defeated*, I been told galactic nubia has been planted in the seeding of the 4 corners, I been told that greater nubia must be carried in the soul,

2:8:6: *folk come to me when their souls are weary,* want to lay right down and die, I sprinkle a little of rickydocs special blend in they path, tell them dont get weary, children, redemption is at hand, when you feel like you got no hope, just spread your wings and fly - geas by rickydoc,

2:8:7: *sometimes you look at the condition of the world today* and you wonder if it has ever been this bad, but we've climbed some difficult mountains, you and I, our struggle has always been epic and we have always overcome, slavery, southern peonage, the movement, win some, lose some, you keep on struggling, it is we who have been born in struggle ensure that in the great gitting up morning all gods folk will be free,

it is difficult but not impossible to dance on
one leg - play on playa, a luta continua,

demoja

2:9: hoodoo fortitude
help me, mariahdessa, help me take this hammer, hoodoo tough

2:9:1: *fortitude:* the fine art of taking the hammer, every true achievement require fortitude, the ability to endure discomfort while positioning yourself for your next move, the ability to sustain a campaign until it succeeds, the ability to beat a straight lick with a very crooked stick, no matter how twisted the path, how rocky the road, you can always make progress, dont let nobody tell you different, you can always maintain,

2:9:2: *it is patience that help us bear trial and tribulation,* the certitude of hope, small tasks require some patience, great tasks require great patience - some conditions must be accepted, only a change of attitude will do, if you cannot control your environment you must control yourself, the only transformation you can truly depend on, sometimes all you can do is endure,

2:9:3: *who the lame claim he know the game,* where did she learn to play, Id like to tell how I fell to the tricks life sent my way, if you gather round I will run it down and unravel the mystery, when the night turn bright and the jungle screams the game will stalk its prey, when blood been shed and words been read the weak are doomed to pay, but its all in the game, no one to blame, knew the rules when I sat down to play, you go down hard, you play your part, crying o my god, what a bitter bitter cup,

2:9:4: *in de geas of rickydoc I would my generations meet any challenge*, finesse any condition, flourish under any circumstance, the hoodoo way never acknowledges defeat, defeat just another move to be leveraged, nothing can hold down a determined folk, no hammer can break you, in de geas of rickydoc there is always a way - and if there aint one, make one - *I am weary, lord, but I will not fall, I been broken but I will not crawl,*

2:9:5: *courage:* a willingness to step out of your comfort zone, to go beyond what you know, to confront the unknown, courage comes not from the lack of fear but in spite of it, the willingness to face your demons instead of hide from them - only by confronting demons can you master them, take their power and make it yours, sometimes courage require action, sometimes courage is knowing when not to respond, courage is always an act of faith - *courage* - just saying it makes it so, it is a word of power - *courage* - says the hourglass drummer, come sing kumbas song, she who was captured young by cekura the lionman, she who was beaten when she refused to carry his lioncubs, when she finally escaped she carried a full measure of bitterness in her nationsack, 1st thing she do she ask the villagers, who is the strongest hunter among you, teach me what you know - *courage* - sings the hourglass drummer, come sing kumbas praise, she who wears the lions mane, horse of mariahdessa, she who needs no title,

2:9:6: **Im told of a king once thrown from his horse** and lost a toe, the babajohn healed him up and said its all good, and the king was furious, no, it is not all good, he said, and drove the babajohn into exile, and so the king does without guidance until the day he is captured by tribal folk trussing him up for sacrifice when they see the missing toe and declare him unfit, upon his release he sent for the babajohn and asked for clarity, whereupon the babajohn told him - *there is something of value in every adversity if you season it with time and perspective* - thenceforth the king was acclaimed for his wisdom and no one was surprised when he died with a satisfied murmur - *its all good,*

2:9:7: **one day the gods notice a raging forest fire** and they take note of a raven flying from nearby lake with a beak full of water, they watch her race ahead of the flame and drop her full beak on it before flying back, feathers singed and smoking, to the lake for another, and then they see the nest she is trying to save, beak by beak, and tears of divine compassion become lifesaving rains,

when the hardtimes come
shalabongo, my children

hold on

2:10: hoodoo blues
come baba abioto, sing a blues for
me, carry me through, make me new

2:10:*1*: *folk think the blues about feeling bad*, au contraire, the blues about getting through the blues, turning adversity into power, finessing the hardtimes and celebrating the goodones, everybody get the blues, cause life is hard & sometimes you lose, you get weary in your soul - blueswork encompass the finesse of tribulation through transformation, the redemption component that drive afroam culture at its best, get to sanging about laying your head on some lonesome railroad iron and soon enough you into the music of it and you not feeling bad no more, you making art, you sanging your heart out, you have transformed trouble into power, tribulation into art, you flow,

2:10:*2*: *the hammer is transformed into strength through reflection* & spiritual alchemy, by landing stronger than whence you came, where I come from the blues are a way, when blackfolk were not allowed to read and write during the lean years of slavery, it was the blues carried the tradition, it was the blues made a way when there was none,

2:10:*3*: *august wilson recount what he consider his artistic revelation*, when in the fall of 1965 he put on an old 78 rpm, nobody in town can bake a sweet jellyroll like mine, by bessie smith, and say it transformed him - *I saw the blues as a spiritual conduit that gave spontaneous expression to the spirit that was locked in combat and devising new strategies for engaging life and enlarging itself. it was a true and articulate literature that was in the forefront of the development of both character and consciousness. I turned my ear, my heart and whatever analytical tools I possessed to embrace this world, I elevated it, rightly or wrongly, to biblical status,*

2:10:*4*: *dead on stroke of midnight* and the bluesman got a deal to strike, want to play guitar like nobody else play guitar and been told to be here if he want to cut the deal with scratch, so the bluesman not but so concerned when the big black man appear but also he know you got to be alert when old scratch hunting souls, you him, he ask and his satanic majesty is amused, who else gon be at the crossroads dead on midnight, son, Im in the market for souls this fine evening, you talking or you selling, o Im selling, robert johnson say, so old scratch tune up johnsons guitar for him and pass him a sack of songs, you gon be able to ride these here songs to lasting fame and fortune, son - but the sack feel a little light to johnson, you trying to trick me aint you, he say, how many songs I got in this here tiny little sack, well now, son, say scratch, you have lived life a little too hard, your soul damn near mine already, you aint gon have time for more than this less you change your ways, scratch pause then but when johnson dont reply he continue, your soul aint worth no more than these 29 songs here but thats all you need if they good ones,

2:10:5: *any blues will do but for hardtimes call on ekpe abioto,* de high priest of memphis, opener of gates and the only practitioner ever knowed to best old scratch at the crossroads – *no demon can stand before the drums of abioto* - to call down abioto I suggest percussion, but any soulful music will suffice,

2:10:6: *witness blues mama etta james,* older she got, closer she got to ancestral the bluesier she got, a study in endurance, rolling onto stage in her wheelchair, still shouting the blues,

2:10:7: *where I come from the blues are a way* that will open any path - *if your load is heavy, come share it with me, if your burden wear you down, if your soul is weary, bring it here to me, I will help you bear this load, I will set your spirit free* - whatever your condition the blues will see you through, aint no condition a good blues cant handle,

demoja demoja demoja
all my blues, all my love

2:11: hoodoo agency
come mambo adero, come dance on the winning hand

2:11:1: *agency, the fine art of making things happen,* anything worth having you have to work for it, the fruit of planning / execution / perseverance, always have a plan, a clear plan of action with doable steps to be sustained with minimum maintenance, to be adjusted and recalibrated as necessary, every move mission critical - living out your dreams will cost you, but coasting will cost you, too - talk less, do more,

The Hoodoo Book of Flowers

2:11:2: action is the final component of wisdom, knowledge that aint actionable just a bunch of facts, a good decision prioritizes reality over illusion, a good decision considers alternatives / capabilities / available resources, a good decision anticipates consequences - once a good decision been made, be decisive, do not hesitate, do not wait for conditions to be perfect, they never are, if the timing is not right use the delay for preparation and positioning, thus when the moment is ready so are you,

2:11:3: understand the rules of achievement and apply yourself to their mastery, be force in the world, a race of doers, practitioner adepts of making things happen - *play on playa, step up* - like the evening confederate guards in charleston harbor received the right signs and countersigns from a confederate steamer, *the planter*, its owner waving as always under his distinctive white hat, so distinctive in the gathering dusk the guards did not note that it was actually trusted slave pilot robert smalls, having convinced the black crew to run for it, smalls picked up his family and 8 other runaways before selling the planter to the union, along with confederate navy codes, signs and countersigns - with his share of the prize money he bought the plantation of his slaveowning father, who had pampered him so that his mother sent him into the fields so he would never forget that he was a slave, not a son,

2:11:4: as a hoodoo adept climbing ladders of power, you will sometimes find yourself out of your league, intimidated, ignorant of the rules of play, remind yourself, *I am high hoodoo, I am the power here,* no longer intimidated by folk who are, beneath the props, no greater than I - each rung you must learn the rituals of your new circumstance, start slowly, be steady, the observer, maintaining a low profile until you know who the players are, how the game flow, read the books, decipher the codes, attend to the rituals, get bloodied in the arena, this is a skill that comes only with the doing - the tale is told of the zen master of the mountains who was invited to court to advise the emperor, at court he is dismayed to find himself intimidated by the nobles grace, their beauty, power, and ease, he withdrew to the mountains to meditate upon the essential until he was unintimidatable - *I do not agree with this strategy, Ida hung out at court till I was myself a player, maintaining a low profile until I had mastered the rules of play,*

2:11:5: to move an organization be willing to serve it, position yourself as a significant / indispensable factor through the quality of your work and your commitment, always be mission critical, an institutional resource, sometimes you a chief, sometimes you a spear carrier, do them both well, the team is depending on you,

2:11:6: some victories not really victories, victory changes things, false victory only changes the illusion of things, victory aint victory till adero dance - the cargo cults of melanesia formed companies that marched back & forth with sticks and thought it would cause airplanes to parachute in mana / cargo from heaven, cargo cults like the marching rule of the solomons evolved into acculturated instruments of empowerment, whereas cults like the taro movement were primarily magical, marching around in formation with sticks on their shoulders & calling it power - *stay in the briar patch, brer rabbit, you aint ready,*

2:11:7: in the days of slavery far more folk chose accommodation over resistance, they forged lives, raised families, built institutions, made a way out of no way, who to say who showed the most courage, good game will satisfy folk like you and me but most folk just want to live the good life with their families, who can deny them this, is this not the essence of struggle, to forge a people capable of finessing increasingly complex societies, capable of successfully manipulating their society, making it work for them, illuminating it, making it serve the greater good, buncha middle class achievers - rest of us are warriors in the struggle that will never be won, the alleviation of misery / hunger / poverty / conflict / war / inequity / these things are part of the human condition and will always be with us, alleviated only by sturdy champions of the social contract, spreading hoodoo blessings whensomever you can, win or lose humanity at its best, *shalabongo*

the best victory is over your own nature,
only by mastering yourself can you
master the world, be the mojo

demoja

2:12: hoodoo fortune
la nunez, obeah queen of fortune, come
smile upon me, your chosen one

2:12:1: the hoodoo dance of fortune, the only thing certain is that fortune will change on you, the good turns bad, the bad turns good, fortune smiles, fortune frowns, all the power in the world still needs fortunes favor, no one is exempt, the saint / sinner / wise / fool / all must bow & bend to fortune and the random factor, want to accept the blessings got to take the hammer as the invitation to growth that it is, they a matching set,

2:12:2: *fortune favors those who prepare for it*, a free floating readiness that recognize fortune in its early stages, be attuned to the roots of things, when opportunity calls its too late to prepare for it, prudence anticipates adversity and positions itself accordingly, good luck or bad, be prepared to finesse them both, be prepared to endure,

2:12:3: *fed by gold and the spears of mounted warriors*, sunjata built mali on a bed of ghanas bones before it fell in its time to the songhay, it was the end of an era when the songhay capital of wagadu fell, shields and spears useless against the guns of the moroccans, the scribes of timbuktu will tell you their defeat was in the botched sacrifice of a goat, but rickydoc say be on the cutting edge or fall to them that is - the songhay were defeated, the wakauri eviscerated, ahmad baba al massuli al timbuktu exiled and lo and behold the moroccans tried to burn the books of timbuktu, what is it with folk trying to burn the books of timbuktu,

2:12:4: *but the gods refuse to let the glory of the songhay leave this world bereft* and every morning the eternal city of gao floats into the clouds, every morning the bullets of the moroccans fall short and gao the eternal escapes unscathed, to rise again the next morning and the next unto eternity, that glow you see in the middle of the sun, gao the eternal, do not gaze upon her long, the sun will blind you,

2:12:5: *empires rise and empires fall*, it has always been this way, witness the march of the bantu, a mfcenic whirlwind change everything in its path, wiping out whole peoples and forging new ones, empires rise and empires fall, it has always been this way but when the ansar dine tried to smash the shrine of sidi yahia all they destroyed was the building, if we, the sons and daughters of slaves, cannot free slaves what good are we, the bella and the hal-pulaar await the conch horns call, fortune favors the committed,

2:12:6: back in the day brer rabbit had 5 feet, the 5th foot mammy bammy, the witch rabbit, gave him, he attribute his success in life to that foot and when he lost it he braced for the bad luck that wasnt long in coming, before you know it he cant keep love or money and anything that could go wrong went wrong, so by and by he got himself to mammy bammy big moneys place out there in dismal swamp, lost that lucky foot you gave me, he told the witch rabbit, need me a replacement, mammy bammy look about and see brer rattler sunning himself on a rock, you bring me brer snake there all tied up, she say, and we will see about that lucky foot, so brer rabbit he ponder a moment before getting a rope and a stick and he go over to brer snake and say, excuse me, brer snake, but mammy bammy claim you not but 3 feet long and I say no, he at least 4, do you mind stretching out along this here measuring stick so I can tell, not at all, brer rabbit, say the snake, personally I believe I am at least 5 or more, but soon as he stretch out brer rabbit rope him to that stick and bring him over, apologizing most profusely, mammy bammy release brer snake and mollify him with the offer of free consultation every time he shed his skin, which is of course why they do it - after he slither off a satisfied customer, mammy bammy say that took you all of 5 minutes, brer rabbit, if you had luck and smarts too, you would be a danger to all the other animals, you get to keep one, you choose,

2:12:7: Im told a poor and lonely man once decide to walk to heaven and ask for redress, along the way he meet a wolf and a good woman, both of whom have a question for god, the wolf ask why life got to be so hard, Im starving, the good woman tell him to ask god whenever will she find a good man, he agree to do so, but before he get to heaven he rest at the foot of a riverbank bottletree that is parched and stripped of leaves, tree tell him to ask god why cant I draw moisture from my own river, so when dude get to paradise he ask god for answers, god give him replies to the wolf, the woman, and the tree and say you will find your own fortune at the end of your journey, so he return home the way he came, to the tree he says god told me there is a pot of gold under your roots, that is why you cannot get nourishment, but when the tree begs him to dig up the gold, he says that he does not have time, my fortune awaits, to the good woman he says a good man will be sent to you soon but when she asks him if he will stay for lunch he tells her no, I must be about my fortune, to the wolf he says a fool will come along directly, a silly man who has passed up both wealth and love just to feed your hunger,

2:12:8: always got to be prepared to take the hammer. long as you stay on game you good, remount the board, stronger, more informed, this resilience is what transforms misfortune into fortune, for fortunes favor we will call on la nunez, legba can turn on you but la nunez de obeah queen, never will, to call down nunez a book that mean something to you, and mangoes, nunez like mango, who dont like juicy sweet mango, and moko jumbie, a good stiltwalker make any day holy,

2:12:9: my luck is no greater than any other, I am just more prepared to see / finesse opportunity than most, more prepared, perhaps, to take advantage of the swings of fortune, a freefloating awareness in constant adaptation to evolving circumstances, when moments of opportunity and / or challenge strike, finesse them in total mastery of the cosmic wave,

fortune smiles
all my love

demoja

2:13: hoodooing transgression
stagolee stagolee, step back, stagolee

2:13:1: transgression: the wild thing we chain and repress, transgression and desire, we have, all of us, done things for which we are ashamed, if we say we are without sin we deceive ourselves and the truth is not in us, we are all capable of bowing to our particular demons, thats what make a demon a demon, a shape shifter hidden deep beneath unacceptable thoughts and inexplicable behavior, whispering songs of expediency, crawling along the low road when you could have gone high - *wondering who is this person, surely that aint me,*

2:13:2: dont judge yourself too harshly for transgressive thoughts, your thoughts are not you, the brain is hardwired to consider all the possibilities, thats what brains do, its you that decide which impulses are pertinent to the great soul you aspire to be - understand human weakness in yourself and others, young conjure, how you gon be a spiritdoctor if you lack generosity of spirit, no such thing as a perfect soul, generally folk not evil, they just weak, everybody struggling,

dont judge souls too harshly, we here to
grow and learn, we meant to be flawed

2:13:3: avoid doing anything you do not want known, everything comes to light and your soul knows when it has been stained, be willing to admit mistakes, to apply correction and restitution - gon have to struggle with the demons of desire and transgression all the days of our lives, when you fall off the path, dust yourself off, get back on track, do better, there is always redemption if it is sincerely chosen while the fool falls into a hole and keeps falling and falling until they are never seen again,

2:13:4: testimony by dr. english, (hrc&w): *I get off sometime, I gets a doing and dissipating and my power goes out on me,*

2:13:5: back in 1895 the globe democrat of st louis featured a story about the shooting death of one william lyons at curtis saloon by the notorious gangsta, stackolee, born veiled and double jointed, day he was born conjure woman told his mama, your double jointed baby gon come to a bad end, 1st thing stackolee did sold his soul to the devil for a stetson hat worn ace deuce quatro, article say he shot billy lyons with a 30 odd special on a 44 frame, shooting tombstone bullets wid de ball and chain, say he was executed right away but when he got to hell he threw such a fit they sent him back with a little note said get him out of here before he murders us all, since then he been caught between the rock and the hardplace, raging about the way of things and worrying at folks souls whenever he can, the elders say - s*taggerlee staggerlee, step back, staggerlee* - is a mantra that will free you of any demon,

2:13:6: transgression is sometimes transformative, the artist, the visionary, the guide, the activist, the protester willing to pay the cost, justice is a more flexible plane than law, judge any move by its value to the greater good, the ascensionist is not afraid of the disapproval of various audiences if the vision is clear, according to the griots code you should always be prepared too speak truth to the people, even and especially when they dont want to hear it,

2:13:7: to transgress once, maybe twice, is part of the human condition, you must know the demon before you can name it, to transgress repeatedly is to abandon the way, apply the withering death to unacceptable internal dialogue, do not fight it, to worry at transgression only empowers it, observe it, amused, watch it move on through - finessing demons is an art, once you name the demon it should no longer have power over you, if that fail, call on me, malignant forces can not go past a bonded crossroads, when you cross over drop four coins and call on me - *guaranteed* - aint no condition I cant handle,

2:13:8: the struggle against evil, within and without, is forever, you must always be capable of peering into your own shadows, it is the nature of evil to hide in the presumption of grace, it is our imperfection that makes us human, whats fatal is to hide from error, the strong move is to face error, acknowledge it, incorporate the lessons of it - it is said of the babajohn he never committed the same error twice,

2:13:9: redemption is at hand, come stronger next time, rickydoc understands, rise up, children, shake the devil out your soul,

demoja

2:14: hoodoo redemption
whatever your condition you can
always call on mama rue

2:14:1: for every transgression there is the possibility of redemption, awareness of the wrong is the first step, the ascensionist acknowledges error as an act of ritual purification, getting your mojo on,

2:14:2: have you heard the tale of a rich woman with no heart who one day came upon a beggar who had once been a thief but having recently delivered a daughter was now trying to go straight, the rich woman was so moved that every week she had a package of food and essentials delivered, deciding that was not enough, she gave the beggar a good job with benefits so she could take care of her young family without stealing ever again - by and by the rich woman died, when the heavenly haints in the judgment hall brought out the scale of maat and put her good deeds on one side and her sins on the other the sins far outweighed the good, the haints of heaven shook their weary heads while reaching for the switch that would send her screaming to the pits, she closed her eyes in anticipation but when nothing happened she opened them again and saw that the scales were balanced, you were about to go down, the high haints of heaven explained, when a thief stole in and took away enough sins to balance you out,

2:14:3: if I hide from my sins / flaws / weaknesses I can not grow past them, they have no purpose, confession sanctifies us, transgression humbles us, keeps us honest and tolerant of others, provides for the generosity of spirit that exalts us - restitution demands that those who have been harmed be made whole, if unable to do so then pass the blessing on, only in this manner can you be redeemed in de geas of rickydoc, neither god nor I will ask more than you can give,

*2:14:4: **when possible impose transformative justice** for violators of community mores, justice that seeks to reincorporate the violator into the community, there are, however, some transgressions, lets call them mortal transgressions, that are difficult for even me to absolve, murder, child abuse, war crimes and the like, might have to seek your redemption somewhere else, rickydoc gon cast you out,*

*2:14:5: **it takes great strength and power to forgive**, it appears the weak are incapable of this feat, those who have transgressed & those who seek redemption, here is where you should be, disputes and quarrels, lay them before me, we will not feed wars of no consequence, we will drink again and again from the cup of grace, come walk with me,*

*2:14:6: **I claim juneteenth,** picnics, parks, backyards, cultural centers, performances, stories of struggle, a reading for the new year, I see drummers, dancers, poets, stiltwalkers, I see processions to the waters in the name of sweet queen chilly bee, a moment for my patron haints, zora neale / david walker / gullah jack / doris jean / and the babajohn, I see de great gitting up morning all over again, I see bolls of cotton sanctifying the ground, flowers for yemeya, watermelon for legba, brown tennessee sipping whiskey for the conqueror, a day of celebration and healing, de cleansing, anytime anywhere folk celebrating in my name thats rickydocs roost, once did a reading at the ethical culture center in manhattan, under a sign say wherever folk meet to seek the highest that place is holy ground, mama rue rule,*

*2:14:7: **bring your high john the conquer root**, get it fed, in return I ask rickydocs gift, no violence on my day, nothing but love and community, all beefs on hold, today everybody under my protection, celebrating life and struggle, telling you*

The Hoodoo Book of Flowers

remember when stories, gathering folk around the sacred fire and providing the visions without which the people will perish, and while you at it do a libation for uncle tom, check the text, did what he could when he could, we dont ask no more than that of nobody - *now judge thomas, thats a different kind of tom, a traitor to the race nobody can deny, whose name shall be writ small, if at all, in the great black book of generations* - but uncle tom, show some love, do what you can when you can, today you the people I have dreamed you would be, humanitys living ancestors, gods true chosen, *rise up children, shake the devil out your soul,*

demoja

3ʳᴰ MOVEMENT: LIFEWORKS
*listen & learn & live forever
in de geas of rickydoc*

3:15: hoodoo youth
queen mother sha ron, watch over my generations

3:15:1: youth is a time of learning, a time of testing, a time of wonder, life just a great puzzle to unravel and master, the prize a greater you, a fully lived life - this is a time of great passions, when frivolity is not a crime but a phase, it is also a time of great frustration and onerous limitation, great danger and opportunity, those passions must be channeled while spiritual hungers contend with physical ones, a cauldron out of which you become who you are to be,

3:15:2: youth is when you can expend yourself in experiential play without being held fully liable for the consequences of bad decisions, you still under the guardianship and protection of adults until you have matured into a fully functioning member of society, capable of taking care of yourself, willing and able, even eager, to accept responsibility for your actions and their consequences,

3:15:3: humans are born selfcentered pleasure seekers and must be humanized, there are few things as cruel as children can be, I see a coming of age ritual after which children are treated as responsible adults, ritual up a movement a day, 9 days, let us call this the mojation, childhoods graduation, there is no one that I trust more to watch over you during this critical period than queenmother sha'ron, she like flowers, bonsai, bits of raw iron.

The Hoodoo Book of Flowers

3:15:4: according to baba manetheo, scribe in the house of life, the 1st 7 dynasties of egypt were dynasties of the gods founded by ptah, creator god who thought the world, spoke it in a word and then it was so - chaos of the gods reigned until menes the builder united the two egypts under the 1st human dynasty at memphis, city of menes,

3:15:5: according to baba chancellor williams, scribe in the house of life, it was blacks from the south built the holy cities of memphis, napata, meroe, wo'se, nowe, khartoum, and thebes to the heartbeat of the nile, o egypt / nubia / kush / ethiopia / axum / o wonders of the ancient world, greek legends claimed ethiopians had bows none other could bend, that blacks were the most just of people, that the gods dined with them twice a year, the prophet isaiah claimed ethiopia was a nation dreaded near and far, a nation strong and triumphant, is there any wonder the rasta found god there,

3:15:6: when you young you still got choices, life will tend to lock down your options, keep an open mind as you explore life and rack up experiences, there are options beyond what you can possibly imagine at this stage, be open to stumbling up on a passion at any age - mostly this come from learning / accepting who you really are, you will soon realize, all you can do is be you,

3:15:7: treasure the years of your youth, live hard and dance on the cutting edge, live so hard you dont regret its passage, seek out experiences that carve out the great soul I would you be, at every crossroads the question must be, is this my Fa, is this my destiny - when time come to put all these youthful things aside you will have built a good foundation for a fully lived life, conscious and aware, an old soul in a new body, what a blessing,

all my love

de moja

3:16: hoodoo family
eloise ross flowers - on this rock I stand

3:16:1: family, your greatest strength, your greatest challenge, humanitys primary survival mechanism, healthy families are in a constant state of adaptation, maintaining ongoing communication about the difficult things, managing inevitable family tensions - best make time for family so when you in need family makes time for you - osifekunde of ijebu, a brazilian slave, went to france with his master and became a sensation, the french offered to send him home to africa but he returned to brazil as a slave to be with his son again, whereupon he and said son slipped away from both master and the historical record,

3:16:2: when you find the right mate, marry, chose a mate who is utterly devoted to you, who demands of you your very best, do not hesitate, stepping away from your birth family and starting your own is a critical rite of passage, lifelong companionship a blessing you must purchase with commitment, in de geas of rickydoc aint nothing quite like building a family - as to what that family look like Ima leave that to you, if it works it works and no telling what kind of family mixes folk of the future will blend - before living together as husband and wife, a married couple of the tswana are purified of transgressions and allowed to start afresh - *we are a team, you and I, we will not be defeated,*

3:16:3: sometime it dont work out, be mature and healthy about it, if you gotta go you gotta, do so with love, the tension is over, you loved each other once, move on with some dignity, let time do its thing, if you have children you got to keep the relationship healthy, you might not be together but you still family, good friendship beat thwarted love anytime,

3:16:4: it appear the destinic point of family is forging those generations, mastering the art of forging resilient children, shaping your generations through them, teaching them how to cope with adversity, helping them achieve serenity of purpose and preparing them to be sophisticated achievers in whatever field they so choose, healthy welladjusted adults, sturdy champions of the social contract, give them roots, let them grow, give them wings, let them fly,

3:16:5: you do not get to choose family as you do friends and loved ones, family you take what you get, tensions are inevitable, be a font of harmony in family matters, calm troubled waters whenever you can, resolve family conflicts as soon as possible, be willing to make the 1st move and be patient, generosity of spirit an absolute must - *may the children be forged – goodpeople - may the mature be responsible – respected - may the elders be wise – advisors - may the ancestors be crowned – guides - may the grandabies be many - generations,*

3:16:6: to act generationally is to be conscious of the influence of your actions on your generations, to act ancestrally is to be conscious of the judgment of the ancestors upon your own, try to be worthy of their sacrifices, their dreams, sekou sundiata

The Hoodoo Book of Flowers

once said we dreamed you up, dear regulators, like the slaves must dreamed of us, free, keep ancestral lines alive and well fed, their stories told - perhaps here the tale of two brothers working the family plot with instructions to divide the harvest equally, over the years one married and raised a large family while the other remained single, reasoning that his brothers large family would need more grain, each night the single brother added a little extra to the married brothers portion, while the married brother, worried about the single brothers care in his old age, slipped a little extra onto his - *it evened out*

3:16:7: or perhaps the tale of the sisters aminatou and abalo, the 1st keeper of the line, one day aminatou gave a servant extra food, her sister beat her and her father drove her off, she is taken in by the family of the servant she had fed, it is here the queenmother tells her go bathe in the muddy river, not the clean one, the muddy one - to please the hosts who had been so gracious to her she bathed in muddy water and came out decked in gold and jewels and royal cloth, she return home with many cattle, a woman of means, needless to say her sister went to the queenmother and demanded her riches - only because she was aminataous sister she was told to bathe in the muddy river, not the clean one, but she decide muddy would not do and emerged from the clean water covered in weeping sores, told nothing can be done, it was the wrong river, she return to her village where she is shunned by all but her sister, they return to the queenmother, who says whats done is done, but aminatou offers all her gold, all her jewels, her cattle, all she owns, if her sister can be made whole, so the queenmother gives her back the rags she had 1st worn and says you must both bathe in muddy water, when they do they both emerge healthy and whole and now neither of them own gold but they have each other and that will have to do, *on this spot*, said abalo, *I will build a temple, I will be the 1st keeper of the line,*

The Hoodoo Book of Flowers

3:16:8: in each generation there will be a keeper of the line, the responsible one, the conscious one, I fear thats you, dear regulator, otherwise you would still not be reading this Work, the one person in each generation that takes on the responsibility of maintaining the family bonds, reforging the family vision,

3:16:9: it was the challenge of family under slaverytime conditions cause the babajohn to resurrect abalos keeper of the line, chosen by the demands of the given generation, only the best need apply, the rest must help howsomever you can, thankful its not you - my condolences, o keeper of the line, my sincerest condolences, frustration awaits you, burnout is certain - when you falter call on eloise and / or elise, patron haints of keepers, a tear, a heartfelt sigh, a whispered plea - we *got your back,*

it is not easy to be the hand of
rickydoc - *good looking out*

demoja

3:17: hoodoo knowledge
queenmother ida b, come bless my
quest, bless my need to know

3:17:1: from experience comes knowledge, from knowledge comes wisdom - it is knowledge allows you to finesse life, we all of us start life ignorant, believing what we are told, but experience always questions received knowledge - the scientific method is your default knowledge acquisition mode, theory and experimentation, research and scholarship, with the ability to shift into the intuitive as necessary, a hoodoo education also trains the emotional and spiritual life, why educate the mind if you would neglect the soul, that just makes you dangerous,

3:17:2: the competent high hoodoo is most primarily a scholar, a mix of formal training / experience / common sense / and the spiritual knowledge that feeds them all, the high magician strives to stay contemporary with the inexorable march of knowledge, whatever other folk know you need to know, what they dont know is where you get to play, a hoodoo seeker of knowledge, always ready to revisit your understanding as new knowledge becomes available, mining every moment for lessons learned,

3:17:3: the hoodoo way is one of lifelong learning, sometime free, sometime at great cost, but always essential, lifelong learning makes everything a lesson / evolution, a formal education opens the mind and prepares you to be a functioning member of society but the true student of knowledge knows that a terminal degree just the 1st step, education is everywhere,

3:17:4: knowledge for knowledges sake is a waste of knowledge, what good are theories that have not been tested in the arena, understand the power of the word and you understand why it was against the law for slaves to read or write, 1st thing baba douglass did with his new knowledge was write himself a pass to freedom, the relentless education of our generations has been a fundament of struggle, in a merit society education is probably the most salient determinant for progress, *yes yes I know, calling any society a merit society is questionable*, societies are hierarchical, unfair by definition, always gon be haves and have nots, but if you understand the game and accept

The Hoodoo Book of Flowers

unearned penalty points you can always make progress, in de geas of rickydoc you can always make a way,

3:17:5: knowledge is the fundamental power that feeds all others, control informational flow and you control the perception of reality, that russian disinformation campaign designed to suppress the black vote and elect trump should have failed miserably, anytime anybody tell you not to vote just assume you being played, anytime you dont vote just assume that fannie lou *if I fall I will fall five feet four inches forward in the fight for freedom* hamer is shamed of you,

3:17:6: when the germans captured kilwa and enforced school attendance, education had been a stronghold of islamic practice, masters of learning and book magic in an illiterate african world, but islamic elites, unwilling to commit their own children to a western education, sent the children of their black slaves instead, these exslaves became the educated class while the children of their masters were still herding sheep - when ansar dine and them overrun timbuktu and began destroying preislamic artifacts, abdel kader haidra, librarian of timbuktu, patron haint of books and manuscripts, had some 80 trunks of the ancient texts of timbuktu moved by donkey to safe houses around the city, when ansar dine was finally driven out they had destroyed only some 4000 of 400,000 manuscripts, whats with these folk keep trying to burn the libraries of timbuktu, what is it they fear,

3:17:7: one day a young folk magician decide to go high so he went to the babajohn and said, give me knowledge, show me some magic, my magic, said the babajohn, is I eat when I am hungry, I sleep when I am tired, the young folk magician was not impressed, give me a sign, he said, so the babajohn walked on water and rose the dead - suitably impressed, the young conjure said, now I am willing to listen, but the babajohn was no longer interested in teaching, you want tricks, said the babajohn, not wisdom, but I have come for wisdom, said the young conjure, and that, said the babajohn, is what I have just given,

lifelong education a fundament of struggle
it is lifelong learning set the slave free

demoja

3:18: hoodoo work
come here john henry, come down on
me, let me hear that hammer ring

3:18:1: the capacity for hard work is perhaps the single most significant indicator of success in life, most any effort of worth require good work habits, getting a good job and holding it, achievement of any sort, in particular the institution building I require of you, without the capacity for hardwork no vision becomes reality, accept no excuses for not getting your work done, conditions are never perfect, get your work done and conditions are perfect by definition,

3:18:2: learn how to make a good living in your society, master a skill valued in it, a skill that you enjoy, one that gives you and yours the possibility of a secure future, try many things till you find the one that fit you, something that utilize your particular skillset, that feed your particular passions and contributes social value, let that thing become your lifes work and spend your days getting paid to do what you would gladly do for free,

The Hoodoo Book of Flowers

3:18:3: everybody has a calling, the one thing you do better than anybody else could, the one thing speak truth to your soul, determine what it will take to excel in your chosen field, determine if you willing to invest the commitment / discipline / years / training / positioning - then again sometimes work just a grind, something you must endure, at this too you must excel, such is life - *shalabongo,*

3:18:4: so by and by the conqueror died and went to a place of astounding beauty, a divine oasis in which he found his every desire satiated, his every need addressed, he spent his days in celebration, meditation and prayer, but soon enough he got bored and asked for some work to do, he was told there is no work for you here, everything will be supplied for you, the conqueror said, no work, I might as well be in hell, and just where, exactly, the attendant said, do you think you are,

3:8:5: constantly retool your skills to stay on the cutting edge so you are not left behind in the constant scruff of change, abhor marginalization in any shape, form or fashion, be indispensable, black achievers have always had to be twice as good as anybody else, so good you cannot be denied. the real mccoy, bonified, named after a black inventor known for quality work, *like the real mccoy I demand professionalism in all things,* even black folk dont want to patronize a black shop, I demand excellence and exemplary work habits, I demand pride of product, I want you call an establishment *a colored shop* it is a badge of honor,

3:18:6: slave artisans had to be master craftsfolk, the quality of their work their only security, pride of product made a way where there was none- on the other hand field slaves were hard workers but the fruit of their labor contributed to their own degradation, now that you working for yourself I want you to always do a little more than anybody else would, I need you to root out that slavery slack,

3:18:7: I suspect you've heard of big john henry, steel driver on the B&O railroad, how that old boy beat that steam drill down, *lord lord,* hammer ringing like silver, *lord,* shining like gold, but soon as he won his hammer hit the ground, *lord,* still in his hand, look like he resting but he stone cold dead, folk that was there say his wife caught that hammer when it drop and drove on through, say pollyanne drove steel like a man, *lord lord,* pollyanne drove steel like a man - to call down john henry (or pollyanne if you so inclined) you need only put in a good days work and remember o traveler, great works are not feats of strength but endurance, when you feel like you cant go on, drop the sweat of your brow on that altar and call on big john henry to see you through, *john henry john henry, lets get it done,*

work hard, work smart, then maybe,
just maybe, maybe you got a chance

demoja

3:19: hoodoo love
dearest oshun, love given is love
received, o love come bless us all

3:19:1: everything work better with a little love in it, love transcends all limitation, enhancing both lover and loved, love bless everything it touch - o let us list the many shades of love, love of self, love of another, love of all humanity, love of all tings, love of the game, love that transcends all the above,

3:19:2: until you love yourself dont even think about trying to love somebody else, loving yourself aint easy, everybody wish they were different somehow, self love is accepting imperfection while striving everyday to be greater than you are - loving folk who love you is easy, loving folk who dont is the test, folk you dont have to love, folk you got reason not to love, folk who different from you, strangers of any sort, all humanity no matter their worth, all jah creature great and small, let love be your calling card,

3:19:3: Im reminded of the day a rich widower at deaths gate called his 2 children to him and offered his blessings or his property, the son asked for his property, the daughter his blessing, so the father got his sons commitment to take care of his sister but as soon as their father died the son drove his sister away with nothing but the clothes on her back and the skilz her father taught, that 1st night in the wild she gathered enough wood to get a fire going and keep the wolves at bay, the next morning she packed up the excess wood and sold it, same same the next day, then she hired folk to gather wood with her, paid good wages and health benefits before branching out into fuels and futures, by and by the local prince, in need of a business manager, contracted her to take care of the palace finances and, as these traditionalated tales go, they fell in love and married and ruled a kingdom known far and wide for the quality of its governance, every week time was set aside for supplicants, and then one day her brother showed up with nothing, having lost all his property through mismanagement he had heard the rulers of this land helped all those in need, well, you can imagine his surprise when he realize the queen he had heard so much of was his long lost sister, who when she saw him cried tears of joy / mercy /forgiveness, and so the brother, made whole and thoroughly shamed, left with the greatest boon possible, unconditional love,

3:19:4: love courage is an emotional courage, the willingness to be vulnerable, have you chosen someone you trust, a soulmate who asks of you your very best, someone you willing to court for the rest of your days, growing as necessary to love properly and well - the fusion of two souls as one is difficult and not without its challenges, there are few human endeavors as prone to failure as love & happiness, *choose well,* my friend, a choice that can illuminate your life or destroy it, exalt your soul or debase it, a good mate is the very definition of grace,

3:19:5: romantic love is grounded in the physical, and sex at its best is the most spiritual experience ever, a communion of bodies and souls that will exalt you, but if its bad its really bad, and if you feeling soiled, move on – *everybody got a little freak in them, trick is finding somebody whose freak nature compliment yours* - but the physical wears off, do you move on, go through the hassle of learning somebody new, or do you reach for the transformative, you who have jumped my broom, *(no need to actually jump, a graceful step will do, even better a funky one, line dance across that sucker, show me what you got)* romantic love is good for getting folk together but it take transformative love to keep them together, adjustments made, lives coordinated, natures accepted - recalls me the time wisdom and love was in courtship of grace, to test them she let it be known that she had died, when they hear she dead wisdom decided no need to rush while love set out right away,

3:19:6: sometime the grind of transformative love sends you out looking for the passion of the romantic but it rarely lasts any more than it did the first time, the cycle just reset, to make a longterm relationship work you got to go spiritual, nothing else will do – true romantical story this, also transformational, best kind both, slave madison ran away to canada but returned to virginia to find his wife, susan, suspected of helping madison escape susan had been sold downriver and transferred to the creole, a slave ship bound for new orleans, madison, caught whilst looking for susan, was put unawares on the same ship, the creole set sail with 135 slaves who took the ship and made madison their captain, when the slave women came up from the hold, madison and susan were reunited to the cheers of newly freed slaves, when the crew attempted to retake the ship and were about to be killed by vengeful africans madison stopped it, no more blood, he told them, which worked in their favor when the british in nassau decided not to return them to slavery, so susan and madison lived happily ever after - well, probably not, but at least they was free,

3:19:7: do not try to make your relationships fit a preconceived mold, let them be what they need to be, in de geas of rickydoc love must be flexible, long as it works let it, accept your partner for who they are while encouraging them to be their best, maintaining courtship for the rest of your days, providing emotional support as needed and avoiding deal breakers, that which cannot be forgiven - treating your home like a sanctuary of love,

and when you do find some of that real
good loving, find love in your life, if
you got any sense at all, hold on

hold on to love, children, hold on

demoja

3:20: hoodoo finance
mammy bammy big money, make it happen, make it right

3:20:1: the art of making money, the art of using it well, financial sophistication is a fundamental skill that must be mastered early, without money you are a slave, subject to the whims of most anybody with it, specially them what pays your bills, poor people have no agency in the world, 1st thing we must remove ourselves from this category,

3:20:2: find a way of making money that you enjoy, a way that provides a service to humanity, one that conveys power in your society, I would you be an affluent people, adept in the knowledge of wealth and the proper deployment of financial resources, no flash, no bling, this hoodoo money thing, in de geas of rickydoc using your money wisely more important than making it, you need enough to function in a complex society that severely penalizes marginal folk, you need enough to fulfill your chosen responsibilities, to provide security for you and yours, to project agency in the world, you want resources to bring to the table when the conchhorn call,

3:20:3: mansa musa pilgrimaged to mecca with 1000s of retainers and some 80 camels with 1000s of pounds of gold, so freehanded he devalued gold and laid the mythwork of ghana as the land of gold, but he had to borrow money to get back home - *bling money* - when askia mohammed made an equally endowed pilgrimage to mecca he used his riches to bring back scholars, scientists, artists and physicians to teach at the universities of timbuktu and jenne, solidifying sankores position as a font of scholarship - *hoodoo money*,

The Hoodoo Book of Flowers

3:20:4: most any effort of worth require capital formation, entrepreneurship, building institutions and maintaining them, the forging of empires, nothing of real value can be done without finance skilz and the proper deployment of economic resources, once knew of an ocha house where the leader would arrange trips to casinos, she got paid by the head but her godchildren lost their money and went home broke, what kinda guidance is that, wealth used wisely is conjure wealth, money that serves humanity, witness baba carlton brown of full spectrum, building ecofriendly green buildings throughout africa and the americas, performing a service whilst making hoodoo money,

3:20:5: I expect the hoodoo way to pay its own freight, I expect you to master some skill that will allow you a life of comfort / purpose / achievement / agency, Im partial to artists & thinkers, scholars & musicians, Im partial to making books and making music, Im partial to players in the great game getting paid,

3:20:6: I do not mind support from patrons who can afford it, who understand that the guidance they get may not be the guidance they seek, its living off the sweat of believers I object to, monetizing troubled souls, practitioners that think living a life of the spirit mean you dont have to pay your way, in de geas of rickydoc you charge a client according to what they can pay, dont be taking money off them dont have it to give, in fact I expect you to be the one giving out blessings, if you detect a need fill it, dont be making a living off my believers, I will not abide a thief of souls - *do not shame me,*

3:20:7: once upon a time a courtier of the court come upon the babajohn eating rice and beans and said, baba, if you would but flatter the powerful you would not have to live on rice and

The Hoodoo Book of Flowers

beans, and the babajohn replied, if you could live on rice and beans you would not have to flatter the powerful,

3:20:8: a foul spirit once offered me money to look away, like I would sell my position among the elect for coin, I recall when, having learned of lefthand rituals being conducted around a certain tree, a practitioner of the way determined to cut it down but was stopped by a demon, I defy you, said the demon, but the practitioner threw the demon with ease, listen, said the demon, I beg you, let this innocent tree live and I will practice here nevermore, also I will send you a bag of gold once a month for the rest of your life, and so the practitioner did not cut and every month he received a small bag of gold but by and by the bags of demongold stopped coming and lefthand practices were again held under the tree and so the practitioner went to cut it down when the demon appeared as before, but this time when the practitioner grappled he was horribly burned, what is this, he cried, I threw you easily before, the demon was amused, yesterday it was service, the demon said, today its money,

3:20:9: in the entire brer rabbit corpus there is only one woman of agency, mammy bammy big money, de conjure rabbit, when you need to tighten up the finances 4 coins tossed into any body of water will bring the blessings of mammy bammy big money upon you, it is mammy bammy big money answer the question every generation must ask - how does one live a life of struggle that is yet and still one of comfort and agency,

conduct yourself at all times in a manner
honorable, mammy bammy blessings

demoja

3:21: hoodoo maturity
*lady sojourner, maturitys guide, o font
of truth, come show me the way*

3:21:1: maturity is a function of consciousness, awareness of who you are, awareness of your thoughts and emotions, how they act on you, maturity deploys behavior appropriate for optimizing life experiences, awareness of destinic consequence of who you are and what you do, always conscious of the highroad, soulwork in a relentless quest for your very best Fa,

3:21:2: to the tallensi of the volta, folk are not considered fully human until they become functioning members of society, maturity is the transition from adult supervision / guardianship / responsibility to taking responsibility for yourself and your actions in the world, paying your own freight, maturity is when life gains point and purpose - when you young and strong and immortal you think the world revolves around you but your sense of responsibility evolves as you do, as a youth you fall short you only hurt yourself, falter as an adult you hurt all the folk who depend on you,

3:21:3: in your youth you think yourself exempt from the rules that govern mortals but life humbles you, delivers you from delusion, youthful dreams are traded for more realistic life patterns, maturity accepts what you cannot do and appreciates what you can, maturity reassess just what a legacy is, you wanted to change the world, you barely changed yourself, you take what you can get,

3:21:4: at all stages of life be mature for your age, upon birth an old soul, upon death a young one - maturity is the harvesting, you have established yourself in your field, got stable relationships / a family, you the generation that run things, still healthy and strong, a playa in the arena, top of your game - but wait, just cause you mature today dont mean you mature tomorrow, life is full of crossroads and maturity is always a work in progress,

3:21:5: it is only by grappling with your demons that you become soulful, you must be willing to subject yourself to searing selfanalysis and illuminating selfconsciousness, you must be willing to confront your demons / fears / anxieties / obsessions instead of turning away from them, trying to hide from them - take heart, soulful young traveler, it is only dredging the shadowy depths that you become deep, it is only through digging deep that daylight come, soon come,

3:21:6: maturity finesses all conditions, it is maturity bless every endeavor with serenity of purpose, when all else fails its maturity see you through, it is sojourner truth to whom I will assign this task, what better guide than the sojourner, when she 1st run she just want to be free, when she free she want to be a force, rename herself sojourner, rename herself truth - to bring her down use a flywhisk branched from the north side of a tree and prioritize the hard truths upon which a devotee of the sojourner thrives,

3:21:7: in my youth I was susceptible to folk who questioned the ivory tower life of the artist, in my maturity I no longer question this life Fa has chosen for me, I no longer question my power, I can only do the best I can with the blessings I have been given, I dont waste my mojo doing what somebody else

The Hoodoo Book of Flowers

can do, what I do no body else can, in my maturity all I can do is be me,

remember this, o traveler, to all things
there are seasons, this is yours

demoja

4ᵀᴴ MOVEMENT: THE CHANGES
o let me play the changes, let me
dance on the cutting edge

4:22: hoodoo eldership
queen mother s pearl, life master, pass it on

4:22:1: de babas, de mambos and them, age plus wisdom equal respect, you dont get old without having paid some dues, without having lived some life, picked up a scar or two, physical, spiritual, some obvious, most not, it is years and understanding that ripen the soul, with age comes at least the potential for wisdom,

4:22:2: I believe the key to aging well is to remain productive as long as you can, adjust as you must - as you grow older and find yourself slowing down, you begin to value wisdom over strength, socializing over sexualizing, flexibility over certainty, relying on experience and expertise to finesse the decline in physical strength and capacity, constantly retooling your skill set to stay current,

4:22:3: the precepts of living well have remained consistent through the years, the great ways will all testify, witness the instructions of ptah hotep, its observations on living the good life still pertinent - *o my prince, old age descends, the end of life is at hand, feebleness, childishness comes down and every night I lie down in misery, this is my record* - I say everybody should leave a text behind, a testimony, who you were, what you figured out your short time on the planet, you owe us your story,

The Hoodoo Book of Flowers

4:22:4: be an elder repository of family / cultural history, a keeper of the line, passing family / tribal stories on, building up stock with the folk likely to be burdened with you through the quality of your advice and your presence in their lives, like never before dignity becomes you here, elder respect must be earned - witness that picture of harriet tubman, head down in evident humility, standing outside the home she built on her property in auburn for retired slave elders, still guiding folk home,

4:22:5: go out with style, have some fun, see the world, live out new dreams, try new things, but know, my friend, what you can and cannot do, your power is no longer limitless, hoard your mojo, use it strategically, and know, dear regulator, when to withdraw from the arena - supreme court justice thurgood marshall, holding out for a liberal replacement, said his wife was keeping an eye on him and would tell him when,

4:22:6: dont drift just because you can, elder wisdom is aware of its mortality and the need to make every remaining moment count, hopefully your life has been one of service so when you look back on it there is no bitterness, no sense of a life wasted, the days of our lives are not long, blink one time and you miss a note, blink twice you miss the whole song, live every day as if it were your last, counting all your blessings, gathering up ye mojo,

4:22:7: in your eldership be a font of knowledge and experience, an armchair revolutionary in an anansic web of pushbutton power forged in the days of engagement, these can be your very best years, glorifying in the march of the generations, the victories of your students, the twisty paths of your works, the quality of your closure, enjoy your rest, soldier

- *respect respect* - comes a traveler who knows the road, a traveler willing to share,

all blessings, all demoja
take your praise

demoja demoja

4:23: hoodoo deathbed blues
da baron comes to collect his own,
listen and learn and live forever

4:23:1: the hoodoo adept does not fear death, fear of death corrupts what should be one of the most spiritual moments of your life, the great ways teach that life and death are part of the same whole, the great mojo, the great ways will prepare you for the moment of death, take away the anxiety, make it okay, teach you not to fear - a great way that has not mastered death has failed,

4:23:2: fear of death is normal, consciousness wants to sustain itself, but when the moment comes, as it must to us all, you want to meet it with dignity, death got to be something you comfortable with, the prudent practitioner is always ready to go, I dont want to linger and I would like to avoid pain if possible but whatever it is I will take it, it is a small price to pay for the experience life has been,

4:23:3: life after death is one of the great questions for which there are no answers, in matters of this sort I choose to believe what makes me stronger in life, I choose to believe a life in the spirit makes it more likely spirit will survive the death of the body, I choose to believe this because it settles me,

*the great ways teach us how to
live, they teach us how to die,*

4:23:4: for the bambara the dead move closer to the creator, they become ancestral / intermediaries with the divine / high haints kept alive through ritual remembrance - a good funeral is not for the dead but the living, a celebration which relieves the soul of active mourning & affirms generational bonds, a rowdy funeral is a testimony to a life well lived, the first step in the ritual remembrance of ancestorship,

4:23:5: the specialty of black hermans stage magic was his graveyard act in which he rose from the dead, when he actually died on stage from a heart attack the audience didnt believe it because he had risen from the dead so many times as part of his show, when his fans refused to believe he was actually dead, his assistant decided to charge admission because thats what black herman would have done, some 100s of paying customers at 10 cents a head, some of whom bought pins to stick into the corpse to prove he was / was not dead,

4:23:6: this recall me to the time queenmother memphis captured death, when once he come for a client she was not ready to relinquish and she deny him passage through her door and the baron enter anyway as is he wont, and quick quick he caught up in a hoodoo bind, fixed, no more death in the world, at first humanity is pleased with this state of affairs but soon enough the world was too crowded, folk in need of release was signing online petitions and comatose elders was camping in her front yard murmuring let my people go, 1st she try to cut a deal, look here, baron, what about you only take those that deserve to die, the baron say thats everybody, this aint no punishment, this a graduation, tell you what I will do, say the baron, them that find it in themselves to sing a good deathbed blues, to reach for the serenity of closure, I will let them go easy, at peace with themselves, and me - so queen mother memphis set the baron free, cause a life without death is not a life worth living,

4:23:7: at some point we all have to confront our mortality, at some point you become conscious of the fact that you, too, will die, how do you respond to this moment of illumination, the hoodoo way is to spend your days ever more wisely, to tend to your longgame, I require only that you live a good life, one rich in service, rich in Fa, then death can not sting, least according to tecumseh - *when your time comes to die, be not like those whose hearts are filled with fear of death, so that when their time comes they weep and pray for a little more time, to live their lives over again in a different way, sing your death song, die like a hero going home,*

4:23:8: Im reminded here of that story about a muddy stream trying to cross the desert, everytime it get so far the desert dry it up and force it to retreat in frustration, but on the other side of that desert there is a big mountain damn near touch the sky and that stream just know its Fa is to get to that mountain, but when a voice within say submit to the wind if you want to cross, the stream resisted, *I fear I will lose myself,* but that mountain still a beckoning so stream submits to the wind and becomes moisture carried effortlessly across the desert until deposited in a bracing river of icemelt running down the mountainside into the ocean - *o what an experience the ocean must be,*

4:23:9: who knows how you will meet death, for some a fight is appropriate, for some it is a surrender, the only true preparation for death is the ability to achieve the serenity of the divine at will, the absolute stillness of final alignment with the great mojo - *it is done, pilgrim, sing your very best deathbed blues, and call it a day* - I ask only that you be not afraid, I ask that you respect my teaching, that you die as you have lived, in grace - *do me proud,*

even death don't stop the conqueroo
shalabongo, my friend, let it go

demoja

4:24: hoodoo growthing
robin makeda ragadasi, show me
the way, help me work the changes

4:24:1: nature is in a constant state of change and so are you, at any given moment you either evolving or devolving, nothing stands still and reality is far more fluid than most folk realize, once you understand just how malleable life / character / reality is you accept the responsibility to shape it to your needs,

4:24:2: for every death there is rebirth, to be born again you must first cease to be, whoever you were no longer works, without growthing what point adversity, accept mistakes / defeats / failure as the invitation to growth they are, a new you is forged only when the old you has been terminally discomfited, can no longer cope, be fearless in your willingness to grow, to confront the unknown in search of the greater you, it is in rebirth that you are allowed to reimagine yourself, who do you want to be this time, live out one of your greater dreams,

The Hoodoo Book of Flowers

4:24:3: make your moves in midst of the changes, when reality in a state of flux and fluidity, to take full advantage of this flux you must be a master of many faces, an array of personality cutouts shaped to your evolving needs, a face for every occasion, an occasion for every face, conscious of how you are perceived in social interactions and managing those perceptions, enabling the ability to switch modes with the hoodoo blink, behind the mask we dance, shapeshifters at play,

4:24:4: different stages of life require a different you, practice modality, stay ahead of the changes, dont wait for the hammer to do it for you, too often transformation require the hammer to force it through, it behoove you to finesse the hammer before the hammer finesse you - witness imamu amiri baraka, a lord of the changes, the best imamu was the last imamu, the little old man imamu, wise old elder imamu, mellowed, measured, a study in grace, when you got to make a move, imamu amiri baraka will show you the way, just ask him,

4:24:5: - a chance to grow has presented itself, dont stall around till it's a crises, get ahead of it, reach for a new and better you before the hammer force it upon you, then you can shape it instead of it shaping you - I recall the tale of a woman of power who fled slavery, making her way down hellhound trail when the pattyrollers cornered her and she transform herself into a she eagle what flew off to guinee - transformation at will, a gift of robin makeda ragadasi, a spirit wild and free,

4:24:6: when called upon to facilitate a clients growth you must be careful, souls and destinies are fragile things, young spiritdoctor, and must be handled with penultimate care, even more care must be taken when called upon to transform a society or a culture but the most delicate transformations are your own,

4:24:7: when olokun thought to challenge olorun, olorun sent his messenger, agemo the chameleon, to arrange terms, olokun was known for the vividness of her cloth and from this she drew her power, but when she showed the chameleon the different designs his skin immediately changed to match both color and design, which cause her to wonder, if the messenger is this strong how much more powerful the master must be, she acquiesce long enough to learn the trick - according to ras hu-I - *it takes time for a tree to shed its leaves and put on fresh ones, the tree reaches maturity, it sheds the leaf, if him is rasta him wont drop everything at one time unless him is dead, but as time goes on, him tread in higher qualities,*

the shapeshifters dance, shapeshifters at
play, dancing the shapeshifters way,

demoja

4:25: hoodoo mojo
come sekou sundiata, come bring the mojo down

4:25:1: lifeforce, godforce, the essence of the universe we all share, to do anything in life, including life itself, simply to be, you must have power, you must have mojo, without mojo nothing is possible, no life, no achievement, no nothing, some folk think its breath but its mojo that actually activate the clay,

4:25:2: the mojo represent our direct slice of the divine, when you got your mojo working the good life is effortless, ease will follow difficulty, clarity will follow confusion, all gates will be opened unto you, everybody got lifeforce, some folk got more than others but anybody can get their mojo on, easiest way to enhance mojo is to carry a highjohn the conquer root in which reside the soul of the conqueroo, when something need conquering, in particular your own nature, just dress that root and let it get to conquering, you activate / feed / dress a root by anointing it with your favorite liquor / liquid / scent / blessing,

4:25:3: you want to channel your animal nature, not destroy it, channeling your animal nature is what give you power, what feed your mojo, degrading or illuminating it depending on what controls you have imposed, you gain mojo through ital living / ital disciplines / victories of all sorts / good deeds / service / meditations / good stratpo / the perception of yourself as a force / a master of the hoodoo way / anything that make you feel good and strong, not just good, not just strong, good and strong, like pele bringing ginga down from the mountains of recife, play the beautiful game,

4:25:4: sometimes you lose your mojo, find yourself drifting, dont panic, nobody on all the time, avoid mojo killers like self-destruct lifestyles / bad diets / vibes / thoughts / practice / bad anything that drain mojo, mojo loss often entails shattering your faith in yourself, when you lose your mojo accept a period of fallowness while your batteries recharge, you will know when your mojo returns and you moving through the world with confidence again - *I got this*,

4:25:5: one day brer fox come up with an idea to catch brer rabbit, he slather up a doll baby with tar and set it on brer rabbits path, about midday brer rabbit hop up and say, howdy, friend, he is offended when the tar baby dont respond, he immediately lose his cool / mojo, accuse the tar baby of disrespect and throw a punch, first punch his paw get stuck and he throw another, by and by all 4 paws stuck, brer fox say o I got you now, into the pot you go, under mortal threat the rabbits mojo return with the quickness, do whatever you want, the rabbit say, just dont throw me in the briar patch, brer fox say Ima eat you for breakfast, rabbit say probably best to tenderize me first, just dont throw me in that briar patch, dear god, anything but that - brer rabbit begging so eloquent brer fox reconsider, are you that scared of the briar patch, say the fox, exactly so, say the rabbit, well, there you go then, say brer fox, and he chunk brer rabbit into the briar patch, then he wait for the screams but all he hear is a rustling whilst brer rabbit settle himself, you okay, ask brer fox, Im good, say the rabbit, appreciate you seeing me home, I was born in the briar patch, and the rabbit hop off singing - *got my mojo working, gonna try it on you,*

4:25:6: bringing down the mojo is moving a situation into a crossroads mode, one that changes thing, the prudent conjuror hordes mojo by always conducting yourself in humble dignity, speaking only when you have something of substance to say, a study in ultimate cool, deploying power only when absolutely necessary, the ability to be still is a power move, command positioning, like any other power mojo grows best in the shadows,

4:25:7: the great mojo / the hoodoo way of god / the universal godhead - to each as they are ready to receive, the kind will see it as kindness, the wise as wisdom, the fool as useless, back when we was cubs in the city, babagriot sekou sundiata was the leader of our pack, to bring down de mojo a small sprinkling of sundiatas special blend goober dust open any path,

got my mojo working,
gonna try it on you

demoja

4:26: hoodoo time
come cage we kibiru, come down from killimanjaros peak,

4:26:1: cpt: conjure peoples time, on time, in time, every time, worship good timing, of all the primal forces of the universe, time is the master that rules us all, a ruthless enemy, a lifelong friend - any truly significant effort requires an investment of time / persistence / endurance, anything that happens quickly is rarely deep and lasting, it is endurance that finesse time, it is endurance that give it meaning,

4:26:2: everything has its season, summers for growing things, fall for reaping, in winter one withdraws for regenerative purposes, to be renewed in spring, born again, align yourself with the cosmic rhythms as you perceive them, everything has its optimal timing, your task is to know when best to do what, know when to rest, when to be ready, when to make your move / go forward / retreat / hold on / let go, you know when you dancing through, when its right things flow freely, when its wrong force is not enough, go with the flow, gather up ye mojo, moving in accord with the glacial dance of the stars, one perfect note in the song of the spheres, every day we dance with destiny,

4:26:3: past / present / future is encompassed in the timeless instant of eternity and the word that enables it - *demoja* - clock time is our attempt to master time, put it to work, mind time is times defiance of mastery, anytime you have experienced a sensation of timelessness you have laid your hand upon eternity, mind time can stretch an hour unto eternity or encompass eternity in an instant, even clock time is confounded by relativity - consciousness of time is what has allowed us to harness it, shape every aspect of our lives around it, valiant butterflies living on the clock, do not blink, *tick tock, tick tock,*

4:26:4: act in accord with the demands of the times if you would Works that grow with time instead of being diminished by it, all Works are contemporary in development, it is time and the judgments of the generations that determine which Works are to be treasured / iconicized, if you would Works that establish a dynamic relationship with time you must engage issues humanity considers essential, then master the Craft necessary to create Works so compelling, so essentialist, they cannot be denied,

4:26:5: patience, an intimate relationship with time, an intuitive appreciation for timing, without patience nothing is possible, small tasks require small patience great tasks great patience, patience is not idle waiting, patience is positioning yourself - preparation has been made but you must wait for the situation to mature, do so without worry, fortify mind, body and soul,

4:26:6: time strips away the superficial until only the essential remains, *your move, playa, strike, strike now,*

4:26:7: most any serious project will take years to develop / implement / maintain, be ruthless, be strategic, constantly refining your production / discipline / getting more bang for your buck, mastering time management principles, living by the clock, sometimes you feel good about it, sometimes you dont, what, pray tell, does how you feel have to do with getting your work done,

4:26:8: our measurements of time are shaped by the movements of the heavenly bodies as we have perceived them through the years, starting with the day and the sun, the year and the rotation of the earth, the 30 day effects of the moon, it is the movement of the stars in the sky that have provided our measurements of time, is it any wonder astrology still tries to attune our individual actions / song to the rest of the universe, to the majestic dance of the stars,

4:26:9: time is the prophets true instrument, to think longgame we need temporal reference for longgame thinking, something like the 7 hoodoo ages, each age like a zillion years,

1st millennia, age of terra, planetbound
2nd millennia, age of sol, colonizing the solar system
3rd millennia, stellar age, colonizing the stars
4th millennia, age of contact, or are we alone
5th millennia, galactic age, a star faring folk
6th millennia, elder age, elder race in transit
7th millennia, the seeding, transhumanization

I speculate the seeding reset the cycle on a higher plane, a quasidimensional big bang - it appears I have gone full on speculative here, just following the logic of the destinywork:

crossroads on the hoodoo board of destiny
an auspicious conjunction of useful forces

showtime, shalabongo,
my friend, shalabongo

4:27: hoodoo journeys
high haint harriet of the eastern shore, come see me safely home,

4:27:1: anytime you move away from your comfort zone, away from what you know, you journeying, these life journeys, within and without, are the process by which you find your Fa, we are, all of us, on the heroes journey, what the hero brings back from the heroes journey is a baby myth, a brand new story,

4:27:2: the hoodoo way postulate two souls, the home soul and the traveling soul, the home soul is your personal slice of the great mojo, the home soul is you, the traveling soul is the one what journey forth in dreams / astral projection / conjurations and dimensional work / the one that go ancestral - to activate the traveling soul you must 1st learn, in your meditational practice, to separate your consciousness from your body, be capable of mentally stepping back and observing yourself in the physical - *through magical meditation make it so* - embody the traveling soul - *make it so* - experiment sending it out on tasks, strictly scientific method, speculate, experiment, speculate, experiment - *make it so* -

4:27:3: it is through travel that the young djeli understands the way of things, it is through travel that the young djeli gains perspective on their own realities, a young storytelling nyamakala of the sudanic tribes was expected to travel, to broaden understanding by going from village to village, learning from new masters, other cultures, it is only through journeying that you gain perspective on your own community / world / reality, what the traveler learns while traveling depends on your sense of the significant, how well do you see,

4:27:4: and so it was a young scholar of award winning potential showed up seeking appointment as an advisor to the queen (guiding the strong), the queen told her to make sure she got her full complement of education and return in 7 years, so, she study here, she study there, she is exposed to many cultures, many teachers, many new and wonderful things and the young scholar, no longer young, finds she is no longer interested in advising the queen, it is tending to her students and the institutionalization of her work that compel her now, but the day come she find the queen waiting in her line of morning supplicants, wisdom does not wait on power, the queen told her, true power waits on wisdom and so it should ever be,

4:27:5: see as much of the world as you can manage, young conjure, be a citizen of the world, capable of functioning in different environments and cultures, a shapeshifter, damn near always a stranger in a strange land, life as pilgrimage is a journey without end - in the tarikh al-fettach by mahmout kati of timbuktu we find the tale of abubakari keita II, an early mansa of mali, abubakari felt it was possible to traverse the oceans that encircled the earth and so he sent out an expedition, 100s of ships of which only one returned with tales of whirlpools that had sucked the other ships down, unwilling to believe this fanciful tale without proof, abubakari keita II equipped another expedition and captained it himself, sailing on and on till he fell off the edge of the earth into the whirlpool of the historical record,

4:27:6: at the beginning of each journey, ask the great conductor to see you safely home, she whom the babajohn called saint harriet of the eastern shore, ran away to freedom, decided she couldnt just save herself, and returned repeatedly to lead others down the freedom road, it is said of the great conductor that she has never lost a passenger - to call on the protection of the conductor, you need only a whispered call - *o great conductor, come see me safely home.*

4:27:7: of the traveler I require a text, a road map for future travelers, a glyph astra, a book of horizons, a blessing from somebody who knows the road, somebody who willing to share,

follow the drinking gourd and
you will never lose your way
follow the drinking gourd

demoja

4:28: hoodoo healing
papadoc flowers, let everything I do be a healing,

4:28:1: good health is the only thing in life that is absolutely critical, maintain health and all else is added, anything else you can recover from it, ital health is do or die,

4:28:2: ital living: a rasta riff on vital, ital moderation, ital healthcare and spiritual practice, ital diet and exercise, ital relationships, ital public health policies, ital consciousness and meditational practice - treating your body as if it were in truth a temple, a jeweled repository of your soul, templework cleanses the soul as regularly as you clean your body, purify it, sanctify it, keep the mojo strong,

4:28:3: and you, young spiritdoctor, o healer of damaged souls, I would you leave every soul you encounter in better shape than

The Hoodoo Book of Flowers

you found it, damaged souls are under my personal protection, as are creative & illuminated ones - *every day we are damaged, every day we are in need of healing and renewed participation in the divine harmony* - everybody suffering, young spiritdoctor, everybody in pain, your hoodoo mission is alleviating that pain, clients / strangers / the collective / loved ones all / find the wounds that will not heal and heal them,

4:28:4: when in doubt, merely observe, intervene only in total and absolute humility, conscious of your fallibility, who are you to decide what challenges this person must meet in life, souls are fragile things, young hoodoo, your possibility for harm as strong as it is for good, I require of you a light and graceful touch, tender even, I would you master the art of soulcare / souleasery, I would you be adept in the alleviation of suffering - not only will I not abide a thief of souls, I will not tolerate incompetence or clumsy handling, not when it come to souls handled in my name,

4:28:5: often you just a consultant guiding the client to the appropriate professional care, I once heard it said that half the kids on the south side of memphis still belonged to dr flowers because they hadnt been paid for, I love that line, my father felt a distinct responsibility for the health of black south memphis, he took care of their bodies, I take care of their souls - pride myself a spiritdoctor walking in the footsteps of my father, folk from across the bridge called him a *full service doctor*, capable of using both hands, they often paid him in produce, when calling on doc flowers to facilitate a healing he will take most any offering, and mingus, anything by mingus,

4:28:6: dr jim jordan of manleys neck township, north carolina, was respected by the community / medical professionals / and the police / his reputation that of an ethical conjureman of great power who would not take a clients money unless the cure worked - then there is aunt caroline dye, one of the best, all the blues songs will attest, folk sanging about going to see aunt caroline dye was code in the south for trusting in the tradition, hoodooration at its very best,

4:28:7: once the babajohn encountered a demon rode man who upon him heaped scorn and verbal abuse, which the babajohn endured with dignity before disarming him with a murmured blessing - *demoja, my friend, go in peace* - how, asked a trainee, where you able to handle that so well, the babajohn replied - I *gave him only what I had to give, hoodoo blessings, I hoodooed him,*

websters definition of hoodooing somebody say to harm, to hurt, in de geas of rickydoc to hoodoo somebody mean to bless and heal,

hoodoo them, chile, just hoodoo them

all my love

5ᵀᴴ MOVEMENT: SERVICE
help me know what must be done, help me be what I must be, for those who depend on me, let me be the answer

5:29: hoodoo stewardship
help me, ras hu-I, be the comforter I would be

5:29:1: stewardship is assuming responsibility for the well being of your community / domain / tribe / humanity / all tings, custodial hoodoos have always been responsible for the welfare of their community, Ima tell you like ras hui-I say (if I coulda rewrote it better I woulda) - *thats what love, cooperation and unity are in a society, a comforter, Im a comforter for my people, so I have great dominion and power, glory and authority, but I use my discretion and my people love I, because I heal their afflictions,*

5:29:2: custodial hoodoo monitors the spiritual health of the community and the individuals in it, facilitating every phase of the life cycle - *birth, adulthood, marriage, missionwork, death, et al* - custodial hoodoo can only exist in service to the community, service as worship - in the prophetic traditions of east africa there is a distinction between the diviner who uses their power to serve self and clients, and the prophet diviner who, through public performance, also serves god and community, the prophet diviner achieves agency by providing spiritual / strategic / destinic advice to elites and activists, my warrior clans,

5:29:3: I would you take responsibility not only for your own destiny but the destiny of all jah creature great and small, we have come to understand, as must any counterelite worth its keep, cant just save your own, got to save them all, if its not in you to serve humanity how can you possibly think to encompass the divine - when attempting to enhance the human condition, when choosing your hoodoo mission, choose your targets wisely, there will always be poverty / hunger / sickness / suffering is an inescapable part of the human condition, a battle you cannot win and yet it must be fought, again and again,

5:29:4: Im told when brer rabbit made the middle passage he did not take to being worked like a slave, Im told the day come an overseer in those mississippi cotton fields moved to whip a woman with child, Im told the conqueror was in the sudan when the whip rose but was in mississippi before the lash could fall on her back, lifting her up into the sky beyond the slave masters spite, Im told one by one blackfolk rose out of the field and flew back to guinee, but when brer rabbit moved to join them the conqueror say I need you here, son rabbit, and the conqueror point out all the folk who had forgotten how to fly, they gon take a good bit of tending to, the conquer told him, they have an important role to play in all that is to come, and so do you,

5:29:5: when the conqueror realize aids / ebola / covid19 / whatever comes next / had an affinity for the souls of blackfolk he cry out this is a demon that must be finessed in its infancy, but nobody listens - *the prophets curse* - the conqueror muse that a culture that does not respond to cultural challenges in a timely manner is not a culture flexible enough to finesse them, the tactical / survival response to any cultural crises is to 1st acknowledge it, to monitor the evolving knowledge base and change community behavior accordingly, each one of us doing individually what the collective must,

5:29:6: but thats just defense, seems we susceptible to every pandemic come down the pike, the corresponding longgame should be designed to harness the karmic power generated by a cultural crises of this magnitude to make health of primal importance in our culture, a cultural trait, geas by rickydoc, then we will have transformed adversity into power, worked the counterspell,

finesse it and we stronger for it,
otherwise its just another tragedy,

5:29:7: the sabiny of uganda fought the governments attempts to halt female circumcision until the sabiny elders formed the sabiny elders association under chairman g. w. cherborian to review their traditions, the elders association and the un instituted a grassroots campaign around the medical problems associated with what they now called female genital cutting, they also agreed to write out their language, study their herb lore, and systematically update outdated tribal traditions - *supreme good fortune,*

5:29:8: it would be nice, would it not, to forge a people capable of systematically responding to changes in their political / social environment in both a timely and effective manner, one that enables timely adaptation to cultural challenges, adept in cultural conjuration, capable of transforming itself as necessary and on demand, should have been a way to shape the community response to any cultural hammer - pandemics / drugs / gangsterism / terminal slack / whatever / some cultural authority, some sort of *geas by rickydoc* for when the conchhorn call,

5:29:9: the goal of custodial hoodoo is as it has always been, ensure the tribe survive the coming winter, and all the winters of the soul to come, gathering folk around the sacred fire and providing the visions without which the people will perish - *by god and all thats holy they will not succumb on my shift,*

I will be the rock upon which we stand, I am rickydoc, shalabongo

demoja

5:30: hoodoo community
queen mother turbee, come bring blessings on us all,

5:30:1: community most often refer to a group of folk living in the same area, a place of gathering and communion, home / hearth / holyground, it can also refer to a community of interests, at any given time we are members of many communities, formal, adhoc, permanent, temporary, bless them all,

5:30:2: let us strive in every way to make our communities, clean and safe, places of refuge, where you and yours is safe, places of wonder / mythical import / sacred space - *sanctuaries* - places of uncommon beauty and penultimate grace, good places to live, raise families - *quilombos* - the dinka believe in *cieng,* social harmony, attuning individual desires to those of god and the community, for the dinka to break moral law is to separate the individual from the harmony of kin, clan and people,

5:30:3: whatever has to be done to maintain viable communities, do it, if you on a floodplain, regulate it, you in a desert, irrigate it, need a block association, organize it, need a responsive city council and / or congress, vote your interests, better yet run for office, full service politics, school board to president - if not you, support somebody you can believe in, want to claim selfdetermination got to accept selfdetermination, dont concern yourself with getting credit for taking care of business, dont wait for somebody else to address problems you see - *become the answer,*

5:30:4: good social relationships require ongoing compassion and generosity of spirit, expect weakness in folk, be tolerant of imperfection in folk thats trying, fill in the weak spaces, remember all the times folk helped you, not in spite of your ignorance but because of it, in my time of great need it was mama turbee gave me shelter, in her name I proclaim, where there is discord bring harmony, where there is harm bring justice, always nurture the generosity of spirit that ensures our survival as a species, without which we are but beasts in the field,

5:30:5: the most effective tech of slave resistance was withdrawal to the hardground, da maroons getting loose in the cockpit mountains, the dismal swamp, the mountains of recife, **when zo masa reached zaakole**, he gave thanks, kanikookwe, he said, god has saved us, he poured the water of misadu there & he spread the dirt of misadu there & he placed the rock of misadu there & it is there the sacred tree of misadu grew - *on this rock we build our sanctuary inviolate,*

5:30:6: imagine, if you will, that in the brazilian hell of slavery there is a sanctuary / a quilombo / a *palmares,* it is whispered among the chained, the beaten and the whipped, that there is no slavery in palmares, it is written that wherever you find the oppressed, there, too, you will find palmares, imagine if you can, that in the mountains of recife there is a redoubt of freedom, a quilombo where there is no slavery of any kind, where there is only grace,

5:30:7: every community is to be tended to by a hoodoo hand, empowered through service – custodial hoodoo can only be found in years of dedicated service without thought of recompense, you must prove yourself worthy of community trust - your sense of community expands as you do, what was once local is now global, perhaps even cosmic, an expanding sense of responsibility that eventually include all humanity, all tings, yes we is community, and yes we is we, but they is also we,

whenever my people gather together in my name, that place, that gathering place, is holyground,

nagya borana

demoja

5:31: hoodoo organizing
bless this work, baba fred hudson, grandmaster of the prime directive

5:31:1: the prime directive: always organize for survival and prosperity / quality of life / enhancement of the human condition / the security of our generations,

5:31:2: competency in the dynamics of voluntary organization is the single most effective instrument of empowerment in a democratic society, or any other for that matter, the group is

The Hoodoo Book of Flowers

your basic human survival tech, humanity is a pack animal, the impulse to cooperate instead of kill on sight what has gotten us this far - to do most anything of value require a *dokpwe / work team*, learn to work with & through others, make it worth their while to support you, give them a vision to believe in, a path to make it happen - the success of any group depend on the sophistication of the group members, constantly train / empower / illuminate your team, spread power like glittering goober dust that open any path

5:31:3: blackfolk been organizing since day one, from the african union society of colonial newport to black lives matter, blackfolk have repeatedly tried to organize a black agenda, the prescriptions of which have been pretty consistent, various manifestations of empowerment - *social / economic / political / cultural / personal / communal* - folk know what need to be done, its the execution thats been weak, when you trying to mobilize an entire culture its gon be messy, no reason not to try, its struggle itself that count,

5:31:4: as you reach for power by becoming essential components of mainstream institutions, strive to simultaneously build your own, make them competitive, institutionalize them, build something that will live on independent of you, a hoodoo legacy - building institutions / organizations from scratch most often require lifetime investment, might be easier to repurpose one already in existence, join it, serve it, take on ever increasing responsibility, make yourself indispensable, obligate folk to you, building up points for when you need them – for when you make your move,

5:31:5: in any team environment there will be politics at play, it is the nature of cooperative endeavor, of course there is a game and woe be unto those who do not know how to play it, play or not you will be played - the higher you climb, the more significant the politics, the rougher the game, is you in or is you out, and no, it is not fair, but it does respond to good moves and astute play, embrace the game with a whole heart, dont be all resentful and hesitant, be the player you was meant to be, assume the more you play the better you get, want to be a master of the game got to pay your dues, want to be a playa on the hoodoo board of destiny got to step up into the arena,

5:31:6: cant blame other folk when things go against you, they may have had a hand in it but you the one missed the play, you the one didnt handle whatever life threw on you, dont waste your time being angry & resentful, complaining about the rules, take your licks, process your lessons, keep on stepping, work the comeback - evolve into your greatest Fa and everything that happens, even defeat, specially defeat, just another stepping stone in a life of service,

5:31:7: back when the world was still young, all the little animals lived together in peace and love and harmony till this drought come along and left no food or drinking water, except over there in the clayton field, where there a magical baobab, always heavy laden with fruits and vegetables of all persuasion, and a magical stream of pure cool drinking water - problem is the clayton field belong to brer tiger and the great orange monster was not inclined to share, so all the little animals in the forest was dying of hunger and thirst till one day sister rabbit say aint right one man own all the land, she come up with a plan - next morning brer tiger still sleep, all the animals get in place, and here come sister rabbit with a rope over her shoulder, singing - *lord lord, theres a big wind coming gon blow everybody off the face of the earth, wait up, lord, let me tie them down* - then such a racket like you never never heard, brer bear start beating on a old hollow log, *big a bam bam boogie boom,* and the buzzard and the eagle just a flapping their wings and the trees are a bending and the wind is a blowing, and the little bitty creatures just a running all around, shaking all the bushes, shaking all the ground, sound like a big wind coming, gon blow everybody off the face of the earth, brer tiger say, tie me, sister rabbit, tie me, sister rabbit say I aint got time to tie you, brer tiger, I got to tie the little bitty creatures down, they the ones gon blow off the face of the earth, but brer tiger say tie me, sister rabbit, or I will take a big bite, mighty big bite, and sister rabbit say well, brer tiger, if you put it like that, so she tie, tie, she tie, how about that, brer tiger, brer tiger say I still got a little movement in my shoulder, sister rabbit, perhaps you should tie me a little tighter, so she tie, tie, she tie, how about that, brer tiger, brer tiger say you got me tied up tight, sister rabbit, sister rabbit say thats the way we want you, brer tiger, and thats when the noise stop and all the little animals come standing around, sniggling like folk do when they got the upper hand on you, and brer tiger roar, roar, he roar but he tied up tight – by and by the animals get a little bucket brigade of fruit and veggies going, seeds enough to feed all the folk in the forrest, and whilst they digging irrigation channels of pure cool drinking water they singing they little work song –

this the way we work together, cause when
we work together, aint nothing we cant do,

5:31:8: *fore you know it* they mixing in those freedom songs of the 60s, those classic marching cadences, those a luta continuas,

aint gon let nobody, turn me around, gon keep on walking,
nkeep on walking, walking down freedom road

got my hand on the freedom plow, wouldnt take nothing for my
journey now, keep your eyes on the prize, hold on

I shall not be moved, o I shall not be moved, like a tree thats standing by the water, I shall not be moved

and there will be no more slavery, no more slavery over me and before I be a slave I will be buried in my grave and there will be no more slavery over me

cause we shall overcome, we shall overcome, some day, deep in my heart, I do believe, we shall overcome, some day

5:31:9 hoodoos a hand, 9 hands a band, 9 bands a clan, when folk gather in my name embrace the prime directive: organize, organize, organize, aint nothing we cant do

shalabongo

5:32: hoodoo guidance:
*o queen mother ree ree, come open
a path, come light the way*

5:32:1: guidance is the primary function of hoodoo, helping folk cope is what the conqueroo do - conjuration and consultation - *conjuration is destinic guidance,* conjuring realities into being & shaping the future of humanity / shaping generations / making real into the world that which was not / destinywork,

5:32:2: consultation is individual guidance, helping folk address the challenges of life / dropping knowledge, giving insight / conveying your understanding of the way of things, most consultation just good common sense – *souleasery* - expose clients to truths they cannot ignore, truths that make the unconscious conscious, the implicit explicit, truths that expose dissonance between reality and belief - *basically saying this is the trap you in, this how you get out of it,*

5:32:3: like gayl jones say in the healing - *she really do some powerful healing though and she aint a root doctor neither, she dont need no root to heal. some people say that that is a superior form of healing when you dont need no root to heal. when you just healing people by knowing that they is healed,*

5:32:4: hoodoo always been more head than hand, aunt zippy tull, what lived over in drummond town, virginia, didnt use no cards, no nothing, just told it straight, some clients require presentation, folk dont believe in you aint much you can do for them, they got to believe in your power if they want it to work for them - *now if Im truly invested dont matter what you believe, if I cant Work you I will Work your reality,*

5:32:5: one day stagolee come upon the babajohn and ask, what is the difference, conjureman, between heaven and hell, and the babajohn said dont waste my time with ignorant questions, whereupon stagolee, quick to take offense, drew his pistol, now that, said the babajohn, is hell - somewhat shamefaced, stagolee apologize and put his pistol away, and that, said the babajohn, is heaven,

5:32:6: awakening the sleeper is basic spiritual practice, **protecting the weak** basic human empathy, but its **guiding the strong** that changes things - dont be afraid to speak truth to power, thats what you here for, perhaps you recall that desekoro of kaarta had two diviners, the first diviner sent to scout the troops of segu returned with bad news, the horsemen of segu are beyond counting, he said, kaarta will be destroyed, we must flee - king didnt want to hear that, so the diviner was killed and the second diviner sent to scout segu, he saw warriors as far the eye could see, when he returned desekora asked what did he see, he said numbers do not matter, they approach fearfully, we will take them easily - he was rewarded but kaarta was destroyed,

5:32:7: dont argue with folk, dont try to convince them of what they dont want to hear, tell folk once what they need to know, if they ready you can help, if not plant seeds for when they are, no sincere traveler will try to impose their truths on another, plant your seeds only in ground thats ready to receive it, or as bunny wailer once put it - *you dont argue rasta, you reason it, you celebrate it, you find you own path into da oneness,*

5:32:8: hoodoo guidance is designed to help folk find their greater selves, aligning them with the great mojo so that they employ wisdom and illumination in their lives, it is designed to help them determine their Fa, their destiny, to help them develop a spiritual practice that will seed grace,

5:32:9: when handling souls always err on the side of caution, young conjure, allow folks to find their own destiny, meet their own challenges, find their own way into the oneness - *who are you to know what this soul need to go through* - the practitioner must be able to read in the book of Fa how far you will be allowed to intervene in a condition, you must be careful when meddling in folks lives, much less fiddling with complex cultures and societies, bad guidance and you responsible for all unintended consequence - the competent high hoodoo must be sensitive to crossroads moments in a clients life in which destiny lies in the choice of the moment -

my daily study is to know you when you walk in my door better than you know yourself,

demoja

5:33: hoodoo strategy
*o papa dubois, grandmaster of
the game, come open this lock*

5:33:1: strategy: a plan for achieving objectives and holding them - caught up in the trickbag of slavery the conqueror developed an appreciation for strategy / trickeration, it is through strategy the weak become the strong, maintaining the hoodoo posture strategic (stratpo) / command positioning, dominating the dance and confounding your enemies with the impossible, cloaked in ritual masks that reveal everything / nothing,

5:33:2: a good strategic posture is built on silence and misdirection, roaring lions dont kill no game, the pride must hunt in silence - I recall the traveler who came upon a skull by the road that greeted him by name, my my he exclaim, a talking skull, how did this happen to be, the skull said, *my tongue lead me here*, amazed and astounded the traveler went to the local chief and said I know of a talking skull, I will take you there, the chief did not want to be bothered with such nonsense, if you are lying, said the chief, I will have your own head removed, so when the traveler returned with chief and court to a skull that said nothing at all his own head was placed next to it and the next traveler was greeted by two skulls, how did this come to be, asked the traveler, both skulls replied - *my tongue lead me here,*

5:33:3: *maintaining a low profile gives you more room to play,* overt bids for power raise resistances / hackles / countermoves, I need you to restrain your tendency to wolf, blackpeople, expose power only when you must and never let anybody know what all you capable of, always be stronger than you appear, be still, be dangerous, be capable of deadly harm,

5:33:4: *Im told there was once a woman,* while being pursued by a demon of some power, came upon a collection of uniformed men, each one stronger than the one before, she asked for assistance they agreed to give but when that roaring demon crested the hill they all ran away, so she kept running until she came upon a collection of conjure women, each one stronger than the one before, and said I am being pursued by a demon of some power, can you help me, please, and so they question her, what type of demon, what do the demon do, what are the demons weaknesses, she say she notice the demon avoids water, so they build a ditch and they fill it with water, then they use their powers to bring it to a boil, and when the demon crested the hill, there they were, singing and dancing and provoking, and the demon surged and fell and boiled to the spells of dancing women,

5:33:5: *empowerment strategies should be designed to shape our generations* into the people we most want them to be, with a whole race of people you got a whole array of strategies, a viable strategy of empowerment has to be an overgame capable of coordinating both activist and elite impulses, everybody dont have to agree on tactics, you do what you do, I do what I do, more than enough struggle to go around, more than one road to timbuktu,

5:33:6: *crying about racism is like a sailor cursing the sea because its wet*, surely by now racism has been factored into our strategic posture, a strong people prepare themselves to meet and finesse any challenge, human or natural, kkk or covid19, a weak people just whine, blame everybody but themselves, how you respond to the hammer is the only force in the equation you can truly control, once you understand the rules of play and accept penalty points you do not deserve, (charge it to the game) concentrate on making progress in spite of it all, you can always do better - inch by inch, step by step - handle your business, playa, get your game on,

5:33:7: *I say we consider the security and prosperity of our generations* the prime directive, I say we calm, cool and collected, forever vigilant, deploying a multifaceted strategic posture, some moves bold and strong, some hidden in the shadows, others waiting silently in the wings,

grandmasters of the longgame,
demoja demoja demoja

5:34: hoodoo leadership
dear reverend dr king, show me the promiseland

5:34:1: *leadership:* the ability to make things happen through people, the ability to organize folk and inspire them, you wanna be a leader you must 1st prove yourself through selfless service as someone who can be trusted with power, folk need to know they can depend on you, that in times of need you will be the last one to fold, they must trust that you doing the best anybody could, and that you only call on them when its absolutely mission critical, a trust built up only through years of service - leadership you have to earn,

5:34:2: *if you dont need lieutenants your goals arent high enough,* a leader has to have a good eye for how people play on the hoodoo board of destiny, master the fine art of delegation, the contract being that you leave them stronger than when you found them, empower them with a vision they can believe in, and a path to get them there, walk in visionary gravitas and folk will be drawn to you as plants are to the lifegiving sun,

5:34:3: *do remember, o traveler,* how easily the years devoted to building trust can be lost in one moment of questionable behavior, do nothing you dont want exposed, leadership requires moral authority and relentless dignity, your conduct flawless, your character in alignment with your narrative, always open to self examination, always prepared to acknowledge error, always prepared to grow, folk will not follow someone they cannot trust,

5:34:4: *modularity utilizes any one of a variety of modes as called for,* listen shapeshifter and know which mode is appropriate to the moment, sometimes you have to come hard, sometimes easy - *like this text* - you want to be capable of functioning in a variety of environments and conditions, you dont want to be limited in your functional range by anything other than honor,

5:34:5: *leadership is not something you go looking for,* the only good leader is a reluctant one, duty bound, leadership must imposed upon you, most of the time you can get away with being an observer, a chronicler encased in your ivory tower, choose your battles wisely, do not feel obligated to fight every battle, to right every wrong, do only what nobody else can, it is difficult dear regulator, for somebody who holds duty so dear, but you must learn how to say no,

5:34:6: *good leadership will always cost you,* good leadership always gives more than it gets, otherwise it aint leadership, if you not prepared to sacrifice you need to be in another line of work - I recall when the congo chiefs, thinking they could insulate themselves from the struggles of the folk, cooperated with portuguese slavers until the portugee decreed every chief to be enslaveable if they didnt meet their annual quotas, 101 dead and enslaved congo chiefs later the chiefs found honor in resistance,

5:34:7: *cry not to me, o traveler, of your burdens,* responsibility lies with the responsible, I didnt choose you, god did, write your name boldly in the great black book of generations, each unto self an army, *be the way,*

demoja

5:35: hoodoo governance
calling on de obamas, for those who depend on me

5:35:1: *policy influence is the great game,* state power, everything else is sidegame, only players need apply, policy influence requires social capital, the incessant organizing / mobilization of your constituency, a sophisticated constituency allow you to be a sophisticated player, they understand the longgame, they think in generations, they appreciate astute play and dont leave you hanging,

5:35:2: governance should always be about service, a chance to make a difference, people depending on you, the temptations of governance have brought down many a player, very particular demons await the most stalwart public servant, an overabundance of power, sex and money - *shield yourself with de geas of rickydoc* - the 1st step of corruption is the one you must avoid, the rest come much too easy, in de geas of rickydoc governance is not a road to wealth or power, it is a chance to serve the highest calling, the welfare of the people has been placed in your care, life and death in your trembling hand, nothing more, nothing less, if you dont understand that, dear regulators, you dont belong here,

5:35:3: resist oppressive systems / movements that violate the social contract, especially when they root in your own culture, it is easy to call out the transgressions of others but it is among your own that you must be heard, cultures that have thrived historically have been those organized around maximum development of social capital, those that have been able to restrain rapacious elites, folk like me, predators by definition, there has never been a perfect society, injustice is inevitable, but you can always be a better society, demand that your own culture / society live up to its ideals, spread demoja,

5:35:4: taking state power is easy, holding it is hard, everybody talks good governance but what happens when its your own privileges that are on the line, the true test comes when you must betray your own tribal imperatives in the name of the greater good, when mandela was released from 27 years of captivity he could easily have called for vengeance but he called instead for a society better than the one they replaced,

The Hoodoo Book of Flowers

5:35:5: one day one of the big men of africa heard the babajohn was preaching against him so he had the babajohn brought before him and demanded a show of power, a miracle, perhaps, I do not do miracles, replied the babajohn, I do not do tricks, then, said the chief, you must die, as must we all, said the babajohn, not dying would be a great miracle indeed - the babajohns equanimity enraged the chief, who reached out to strike him and was instantly transported to a strange land where he did not speak the language, had no money, looked different, and had never worked a day in his life, and so he begged, living in doorways until he got a job hauling sewage, until he had a hovel of his own and made a way, except for the time he got robbed, badly beaten and denied care for lack of funds and so forever more limped, and the time a rogue police unit took everything he owned and when he protested he was jailed for 2 years, reminding himself every day, *I am jailed now but in my heart I am a king* – and when he was released he knew the language and had learned a trade, he worked hard and married a woman who loved him, raised a family and knew the ineffable grace of living to a comfortable age with a mate he loved, it could be worse, he often told her when she massaged away the pain in his thigh, and she would laugh with him, not knowing the fullness of his words, and one day she gave him a plain and simple copper ring he always wore, one child died, the pain hurts even still, but the other 2 loved their fathers stories of being a king and tried to conduct themselves with a dignity befitting royalty and life was good enough until the day he reached out to comfort a fallen stranger and found himself standing in his throne room, a young man again, the babajohn standing before him with an infuriating calm and the ruler was duly infuriated, damned conjuror, he fumed, you have taken away 25 years of my life and made me to endure the most tragic indignities, no, my prince, said the babajohn, only seconds have passed since you raised your hand to me, the courtiers of the court all said this was so and fingering the plain copper band on his hand the ruler was cast into deep thought - when the babajohn left he left behind a newly engaged ruler called the explorer king for the countless teams of explorers sent to the 4 corners of the earth, each with a sketch of a woman and 2 children, but what amazed the kingdom most was his newfound benevolence, his connection to the people, his concern for their welfare and his penchant for justice, it is truly, they said, a miracle,

5:35:6: *so obama,* a community organizer frustrated with need for the power to effect true change, ran for office, after becoming the most powerful man on the planet he quickly learn the institutional limits of what he could do, he quickly learn the greater your sphere of responsibility the less you can worry about individuals affected by your decisions / drones - *when in high power you must protect yourself against soul death* - the question when you playing high game is who tricking who, at which point have you stained your soul beyond repair,

5:35:7: *dont be so afraid of being tricked* that you afraid to step into the arena, take your licks, learn your trade, assume that you will win, when you think you ready to dance call on an obama, Ima trust you to play a winning hand,

you are ascensionist, are you
not, power becomes you,

demoja

6TH MOVEMENT: EMPOWERMENT
come bathe me in the great mojo

6:36: hoodoo power
come mambo leveau, our lady of the crossroads, come bring the mojo down

6:36:1: oh ye who would bid for power, if you are of the will this is the way, there are no spectators on the hoodoo board of destiny, all hoodoo adepts should have a strategy of empowerment, a game in play / a hoodoo mission - without power even the righteous must bow, I recall when the birds of the earth meet to choose the species that would be anointed royalty, they choose the cardinal because of its beautiful red robes, but hooded fishing eagles sit quietly in the trees while red tailed hawks protest vociferously, what good royalty that cannot defend itself,

6:36:2: mojo power is personal power, a function of character, while institutional power is a function of position and resources, lot of folk got institutional power but that does not mean they are respected - stripped of your instruments you must still be a force, you must still be a power, this is a function of how you carry yourself in the world, always comport yourself with the hoodoo dignity that demands respect,

6:36:3: at the end of the day consider your mojo, did you gain mojo today or did you shed it, did you get your work done, was your diet ital, got some exercise in, a good deed perhaps, every day you want to be stronger at its end than you were at its beginning, every day you shedding mojo or gathering it,

6:36:4: the command personality is ruthlessly strategic, omnidirectionally coiled. a fluidity in constant calibration with evolving circumstances, command positioning is born in a core serenity adversity cannot touch, be olympian in your confidence, steady under pressure, secure enough to be magnanimous whenever you can, a lifestudy in honor, dignity, integrity - *I am high hoodoo, I am master here* - control of your emotions is the fundament of power, let nothing throw you off your game,

6:36:5: true power is hidden power, use only enough to get the job done - I recall when brer rabbit and brer beetle was headed to the big affair, when brer rabbit said to brer beetle at the rate you going you will never get there, au contrary, say brer beetle, I will be there before you, brer rabbit commence to mocking brer beetle, he say who fooling who, so they get up a bet on who gon get to the party 1st, and before the words were out of his mouth brer rabbit was in the wind, but when he get to the party, brer beetle was already there, how did you do that, brer beetle, tell me, what did you do, brer beetle fluttered his wings just so and he said, my friend, I flew, brer rabbit say what, I didnt know you could fly, brer beetle say aint your business to know what all I can do, just because I go low dont mean I cant go high, just cause I crawl in the dust dont mean that I cant fly,

6:36:6: I have tried to boil the challenges of my generation down into an impressionable word, what I have come up with is empowerment - *social empowerment / political, economic and cultural empowerment / personal / financial / familial / professional / communal* - you name it, empowerment will cover it, basically making anything, everything, better, stronger, more effective, focus - dont care what the condition is, it can always be better, same same when I exhort folk to walk the high road - *can always be better than you are, always room for improvement,*

6:36:7: in my youth I aspired to be a hard man, called myself a hordesman, earlier version of this text was called *black power, the will and the way,* read it in a new ren writers guild workshop one day and doris jean austin diva-bit me, *darling,* she said, *its beneath you* - in my maturity my understanding of power has evolved, it distress me to acknowledge Im still a powerfreak, what wouldbe prophet aint, trying to tell whole societies, indeed, all humanity, which way to go - but it is spiritual power I now seek, more enduring, I believe, less wear and tear on the soul,

shalabongo
my friend

6:37: hoodoo gatherings
babagriot d. walker, let the conchhorn ring

6:37:1: once again we are in the presence of Fa, when destiny lies in the choice of the moment, standing at the crossroad, wondering which way will we go - *when the conchhorn calls all things petty must be put aside,*

6:37:2: I ask you, what is to become of the blackpeople,

do we maintain blackness in a multiculti future in which getting along w/other folk ever more critical, everybody mixing it up but us

- or are we to be some kind of permanent bottomfeeders -
- or do we just disappear as a culture and people, or -

The Hoodoo Book of Flowers

- be a fragile folk, easy to injure / offend, in desperate need of safe spaces

or are we to be a comfortable part of the mix, carrying ourselves with an unassailable dignity, manifesting an afrospiritual culture of illumination, service and empowerment so appealing that black identity is valued, that folk all over the world proud to call themselves black,

6:37:3: - when ngolo returned from exile his followers swore the great oath of segu - *betray us and the 4 great boliw of segu will betray you, may bakungoba not spare you, may nangoloko not spare you, may contara not spare you, may binyejugu not spare you* - when the songhay were attacked by morocco, mali sombo called on sambonkon, chief drum of the 7 drums of the zarma, when sambonkon is beaten no one asks why, just come - when war came to the niumi, the jokadu king, demba sonko, called conch on his allies but it was a battle that could not be won and only kelefe saane came, demba sonkos enemies offered kelefe many riches not to respond to the call of the conch, you cannot win they told him, but kelefe saane said - *I give no less than I expect, I do not ask an ally if he thinks I will win or lose, I only ask him to come, to bring shield and spear, to honor his pledge to me,*

6:37:4: a gathering of sorcerors is reserved for matters of existential concern, hoodoos are solitaires by nature and definition, when hoodoos gather special care must be taken, one wrong move and its sorcerors war up in here, who tricking who, whose reality will prevail, who de patternmaster up in here - remember this, all my conjure clans, when the conch is called all things petty must be put aside, geas by rickydoc, a gathering of the hoodoo clans is always a crossroads,

6:37:5: hegemony tends to the comprehensive, local power is swallowed by regional power, regional by national, national by international, the next order will be a global one, cosmic even - in de geas of rickydoc I see what the elders of kush saw through the door of no return, galactic kush, do not fear, redemption is near in the daylight dream of rickydoc,

6:37:6: a rooster crows while a young man crumples into the doorway of a row house in cobble hill, boston, where escaped slaves have made the neighborhood a precious freefolk sanctuary, dear god, he murmur, not now, he try to draw another breath and fail, had it all been for naught, all the copies sewn into all the linings of all the used clothes shipped south with colored sailors, a written appeal for a slave uprising addressed to a people illiterate by law, he try to force his fading body to rise, be nice to see the sunrise this one last time, but all he can do is lie there, listening to the fading echoes of the roosters call, wondering whatever on earth made him think words would ever be enough - *our greatest happiness shall consist of working for the salvation of our whole body, when this is accomplished a burst of glory will shine upon you which will indeed astonish you and the world,*

6:37:7: baba d walker lives in rickydocs appeal to the colored citizens of the world, my gathering of hoodoo spears, rest easy, baba, I got your back,

one day somebody will get mine,
in de great gitting up morning,
all gods children will be free,

demoja

The Hoodoo Book of Flowers

6:38: hoodoo sciTech
me n you, baba ogun, on the cutting edge

6:38:1: the competent high magician is more metaphysician than mystic, the scientific method is your default knowledge acquisition mode, theory and experimentation, research and scholarship - *question everything* - when you get new information test it against your current understanding, if its congruent accept it provisionally, until it can be further tested, if it doesnt make sense to you park it for further testing, if it doesnt test out you have still gained knowledge,

6:38:2: when science and faith conflict, bet on science, imponderables like god / fate / death are deadly mists of ignorance eroding as natural laws supplant those of magic and religion, god retreats, thunder no longer gods anger but meteorological phenomena we harness through understanding as electricity, science depend on the primacy of causation, assuming on faith that every event has a preceding cause according to natural law as we perceive it, an ever evolving understanding constantly refining itself so that todays answer is tomorrows question, it its only when science fumbles that you call on faith, when you get into the realm of what we have not yet figured out, or that we will never know, thats where you find god, chilling in the gap,

6:38:3: dropping science,
dropping knowledge,

6:38:4: the nature of information is in constant evolution, the printing press changed the nature of wisdom as did the internet in our own time, stay ahead of the technological curve - witness

The Hoodoo Book of Flowers

the black women mathematicians at nasa called *the colored computers* what made the calculations that put us into space, they knew what black achievers have always known, got to be twice as good as anybody else could, got to get ahead of the curve and stay there - when their math skill were counterfeited by the 1st IBM computers they trained themselves to program them, if that aint finessing the hammer I dont know what is,

6:38:5: be on the cutting edge or bow to them that is, when ebele the hunter come to ohanko town with his flintlock nobody in that part of nigeria had ever seen a gun, they appreciated him for his hunting skilz but he was still treated as a outsider with uncertain magic until the day the town was attacked by eberu town and the attackers died, mowed down by the invisible hand of ebele,

6:38:6: it is legba, in his incessant quest for knowledge, decided to measure the length of night and day and found them equal, more or less, not satisfied he attempt to calibrate the cosmos - god deny this 1st attempt at godhead, your knowledge, said mawu-lisa, is not sufficient, this when legba invent science, a new way of knowing, a power that allows us to challenge the gods,

6:38:7: technology frees us from the constraints of nature, the choices we make through technology allow us to shape new realities with unlimited potential for new ways and new things, and new dangers equally profound - science / knowledge / technology is neutral, choices are not, dont come to me talking about scientific objectivity, if your truth dont lead to the greater good perhaps you should consider another line of work, science and technology should always be a matter of service / the enhancement of the human condition / the amelioration of human misery, science and technology bestows upon humanity

105

the power of the gods, the power to create and / or destroy, be careful, o traveler, of what you would conjure into this world, if you would be a god be a worthy god,

demoja

6:39: hoodoo war
come gullah jack, bring shield bring spear

6:39:1: war, what is it good for - well, all kinds of things, actually, war is a fundament of the human condition, you always at war with somebody, if you aint at war you preparing for war or trying to avoid one, parabellum indeed, only a people tired of freedom, a state tired of autonomy, does not practice war, if your peoples are to be secured, if you have interests to be defended, if you want to survive and retain control of your own destiny, then it is war, call it what you like, it is war,

6:39:2: the strong can fight by the rules, the weak must just fight, a just and honorable war is any war you must win - why then fight war according to rules of engagement - so your enemies will treat you &, most importantly, your noncombatants as honorably as you do them and theirs, there is no war quite like holywar for dehumanizing your enemy, the only thing worse is genocide, or slavery - *never again* - even then honor must prevail, war without honor kills the soul before it kills the body,

6:39:3: when possible treat your enemies with a magnanimity that makes worthy enemies worthy allies, if it is dignity denial that makes brand new enemies, it is the bestowal of dignity that makes new allies, but if you cant win them over treat them with a ruthlessness that convinces the doubter - *let my enemies be confounded, let attacks against me be turned back, let no weapon against me prosper* - issa korombe, from the line of mali debo, was wangaari, war chief, so good at war he was named wangougna, mother of the science of war,

6:39:4: at the trial of gullah jack, the geechie conjuror who had given each slave recruit of denmark vesey a crab claw mojo to carry on the great gitting up morning, the judge sentencing him to death taunted him - *jack pritchard, you represented yourself as invulnerable, that you could neither be taken nor destroyed, and that all who fought under your banner would be invincible, your boasted charms have not preserved yourself and, of course, could not protect others* - gullah jack replied - *I did not promise them victory, I promised them the courage to defy their masters,*

6:39:5: the hoodoo posture strategic: to each generation a mission, based on what has come before, based on what needs to be, strategies of empowerment should be designed to shape our generations into the people we want most to be, listen o ye firstborn, to the battle prayer of piankhi - y*oke the war horses, draw up the lines of battle, god has sent us* -same same the warhorn blown by the black farmers of the sahel - *kele dona an kan* - battle has come to us,

6:39:6: wars and conflicts are not won by the strongest force but the most innovative, fighting tomorrows battles today, here we are 50 years after the 60s still doing protest, protest is like a failure of strategy, protest mean youve already lost that round, and reparations, spare me, since when did begging whitefolk become a strategy, the question that must be answered, generation after generation, is just what does constitute

The Hoodoo Book of Flowers

effective activism / mobilization in our times, how does one live a life rich in grace, a comfortable life of power and achievement, defined by unrelenting commitment to struggle, just how does one practice longgame on the hoodoo board of destiny,

6:39:7: if you must war it must be total war, rootwar, the protracted mobilization of an entire culture, conchwar, every possible sector of society, every member of it, each unto self an army,

demojawar,

6:40: hoodoo rootwork
come boukman dutty, lets work these roots

6:40:1: the hoodoo adept attempts to make a significant contribution to the enhancement of the human condition, one that actually changes things, monitoring destinic dynamics and maneuvering to achieve maximal influence with minimal effort, a study in essentialism, positioning yourself so what you doing is the most important thing anybody could be doing at this moment in time, the most important contribution anybody could possibly make - thats what you want, to be standing at the crossroads, working the roots of things,

6:40:2: finesse is the fine art of transforming the hammer into power, using an enemys moves against them, turning one move into the springboard for another, countermoves that turn the trick - consider the one drop rule, one drop of black blood made you legally black, therefore enslaveable, a law that allowed slave masters to enslave their own children, conceived as a liability it has instead increased our numbers and positions us for power in the multiculti future, obama could have just as easily claimed multiracial but he chose to be black - we want to forge a culture so strong / illuminated / magical, everybody want to be black,

6:40:3: colonialism bred its own demise in the rise of the acculturated africans who were successfully able to use its own skills against it as counterelites, the nkrumahs, the kenyattas, the senghors and the mandelas - lewanika, uniter of the lozi, cut deals with the british that, bit by bit, cost him his country but he used the time bought to build an education system that bred players slick enough to win back both land and autonomy - in the play of elites and counterelites, you must be faster / quicker / smarter / more disciplined / better than, the competition has all the advantages, all we got is game, trickeration, the old refuge of the weak manifesting a new level of play - *strategy, the key that opens all locks,*

6:40:4: there are times when one simply must work with the left hand, sometime you got enemies need crippling / confounding, folk say you cant Work a nonbeliever but that aint necessarily so, if you cant Work them Work their reality, every body, every thing got a handle that can be Worked, some worriation particular to them, everybody got demons to bear, every soul vulnerable to being took - in a war of sorcerors the only way to protect yourself from being tricked and took is the absolute belief that you are impervious to bushwizard bullshit, if you susceptible to being tricked you shouldnt be in this business,

6:40:5: traditionally souls are captured by calling the person by name & capping the soul bottle when they answer, I say folk fixing you when they intimidating you / imposing limitation on

The Hoodoo Book of Flowers

you / controlling your space / abuse of any sort / disrespecting you / undercutting you / fucking with your head / somebody close enough to really hurt you, or folk in passing, to whom you really should not allow that kind of power anyway - I say anybody who cripples you in any shape, form or fashion has fixed you, you know you been fixed when you find yourself operating contrary to your character / your best interests / good common sense - *most often the one doing the fixing is you,*

6:40:6: *a brand new slave steps off the reeking slaveship* clad in stinking rags yet thankful to be free of the putrid darkness below deck, soon enough washed, conditioned, oiled and bartered for sugar / tobacco / cocoa / coffee / rum, here come de congo / fon / ibo / mandingo / wolof / yoruba / and de rest - tribes from up and down the west coast of africa, of the many the one god / aim / destiny – lo and behold, de conqueror arrive in a clod of dirt that had all these months been clutched in a sweaty hand below deck, compressed into a hard rock shaped by fear and seawater, basted in shit and sweat and urine and pus and vomit, against all odds taking root in barren carolina soil - *who has cast goat dung on me, what will I do with this dung, I will throw it at the heavens, heavens tears will rain, burnt grass will grow,*

6:40:7: *if you want your Work to be the next step* you have to finesse the best of what everybody else has done, got to outswim them all, like my boy shine, stoking the boiler of the great titanic when it hit the iceberg, bam, shine jump off into the water and commence to swimming - *stroke stroke stroke stroke* - captain come to the rail and say, shine, shine, save poor me, give you more money than you ever did see, shine say money on land, money in the sea, if you want to get home you best stroke it like me, shine swam on, captains wife come to the rail, she say shine, shine, save poor me, give you more loving than you ever did see, shine say loving on land, loving in the sea, if you want to get home you best stroke it like me, shine swam on, so then this shark come up behind shine, shark say alright now, dark meat, shark recollect he aint had no dark meat since the middle passage, right tasty, he recall, shark say wait up a minute, shine, let me talk to you, shine say you must think I just got off the boat, shine swam on – *stroke stroke stroke stroke* - alright then, say the shark, no more mr nice shark, ima bite your ass, shark start cutting through the water - *shoop shoop, shoop shoop* - shine shift into 2nd gear on him - *strokestroke strokestroke* - after awhile the shark breathing hard and falling behind, shark say damn shine, you swim real fine, but if you miss one stroke your ass is mine, shine say fish in the ocean, fish in the sea, aint none of these fishes gon outswim me, shine swam on, and when the news of the great titanic reached new york city, shine was up in harlem, eating a shark sammich, tasty too.

any hammer come your way just begging
o be finessed, always another move on
the hoodoo board of destiny, game on

demoja

6:41: hoodoo longgame
o come grandmaster mandela, grandmaster of the way

6:41:1: the longgame: shaping generations through ideological orchestrations as taught by baba john killens, the great baobab under which we shelter, who taught his legions not only how to write but how to be writers, taught us to be visionaries, what he called being long distance runners, what I call the longgame, shaping generations like the babajohn taught me - I am forever perplexed the babajohn dont get credit for being the visionary he was, but I guess if everybody saw what he saw it wouldnt be a vision,

6:41:2: longgame by the babajohn - *to win this race will require planning, pacing, discipline and stamina, and a belief in our ability to win the long, protracted struggle, we must construct one hundred year plans, two hundred year plans, we must construct institutions for generations unborn,*

6:41:3: when attempting to orchestrate a society you must first identify the accessible handles, everything got a handle, a root to be worked, social systems are cultural configurations that maintain a given social dynamic, the effective change agent focuses on the dynamics most pertinent to the desired new social state and accessible to the practitioners severely limited range of play, study the field till you understand the system stress points and determine what handles are available to your skills and resources, determine what you want the reshaped system dynamics to achieve - once you master the rules of play, any system can be worked, any system can be played,

6:41:4: cause when you work you work the roots of things, every move mission critical, monitoring destinic dynamics, positioning for maximum influence, minimum effort, conjurations that damn near sustain theyself, let others flounder helplessly about, when you move it changes things - my works I consider the seeds of future realities, my ideological orchestrations I consider preparation of the ground - the competent high magician maneuvers to influence those strategic points in the life of an individual or a society when the shape of the future hangs in the balance - destinywork

lets call that working at the crossroads,
turning the key in the hoodoo lock,

6:41:5: my goal is the protracted mobilization of the black community, I see an illuminated people, a people of power, a progressive middle class culture that enables the dispossessed to achieve a certain social proficiency in a world that severely penalizes the marginalized - *each unto self an army,*

6:41:6: when moving a people you must think in generations or strategies are ineffective, frustration and burnout certain, you must be comfortable with the glacial pace of social change and human destiny, phases of struggle come and go, you win some, you lose some, you keep struggling, forging the people you would your generations be - longgame entail developing a lifestyle that is both satisfying and sustainable, a life rich in grace and commitment, power, and achievement, a life that is a testament to struggle -

6:41:7: to maintain command position, you must be the most perceptive player in any given interaction, you must know more than anybody else knows, be more dedicated to the game, you must be the entity with the longest, most comprehensive vision / gameplan on the board, so comprehensive it subsumes all the others and puts their efforts to work for you,

understand the hoodoo board of destiny,
young conjure, and everybody on the
planet works for you, you see

demoja

6:42: hoodoo nobility
queen mother miriam queen mother memphis

6:42:1: *hoodoo nobility,* conduct on the highest plane of which we are capable in our lives, we must at all times carry ourselves with a dignity that demands respect, conduct yourself as a superior personality and you are, a superior personality, a person of honor - if its not in you, fake it until its real, conduct yourself as you aspire to be and you are, dont deal with folk dont respect you, if you got to deal with them assign a mask and control destructive responses to dignity violations, nobody can violate your dignity but you,

6:42:2: *every great way is a morality play,* treat others as you would be treated, the 10 commandments, the 8 fold way, the golden rule, call it what you may, it is instruction in the way of the spirit - whenever the question arises, *do I have the courage to do what must be done,* the answer must always be yes, thankful for this opportunity to once again show what you made of, always conduct yourself in a manner that warrants respect, accept nothing less,

6:42:3: *once upon a time the queenmother received* a big batch of new students who were not impressed with the lack of creature comforts in her hekalu, well then, say the queenmother, you must get us funding, go where no one can see you and rob the first person you see, a few protested, surely this is not the high road, but the queenmother assured them it was for the greater good, trust me, and all but one left to do her bidding, when asked why she had not gone with the others, she replied that the honored mother said go where no one can see me do this thing with no honor, but I will be there, I will see it - *that one she kept,*

6:42:4: *the homesoul is responsible for the shape of your character,* without a healthy homesoul you are adrift in the universe, the homesoul is what ground you in a world constantly pulling you this way and that, challenging your integrity - every loss of integrity leaves you damaged, wounded, to keep yourself whole always strive to conduct yourself as a wise and enlightened force, the next step in human evolution, to be a great soul is the goal of all those who see,

6:42:5: *a true hero is always willing to make the 1st move,* to bear the blame, the conflict may not have been your fault but you the one misplayed it, be open to your own complicity in any adversity, be able to admit mistakes and rectify them, be open to correction - when samba lions tooth went to kill konko boubou, he found boubou singing his praises, the praise singer had left samba out of the litany of heroes but konko respected his enemy and so they did not fight,

6:42:6: *cant be no spiritdoctor unless you capable of handling souls* but souls are very fragile, the competent hoodoo adept must be free of vanity, avarice, and the love of power, if you aint healing you got no business here, it is an honor and a responsibility to be a spiritdoctor in the hoodoo way, to be a patron haint of damaged and illuminated souls - *awaken the sleeper, protect the weak, guide the strong* - to call forth the nobility that resides in every soul you must be secure in your own, do not fear, whenever you falter call on queen mother memphis, miriam de costa will ensure you are bathed in grace, in your times of greatest need nobility is your calling card,

6:42:7: *to war with demons must you become the better demon*, my concern with protracted struggle is that it not demean or diminish us, that it not leave us a petty little people with a bitter little vision, too often the oppressed become in turn the oppressor, witness the tragedy of our mentors in the game doing unto others the same thing that was done to them, struggle must always be ennobling, the longgame is always spiritual, struggles against our enemies must always be subject to the struggle within, if we are to be a better way we must first clean our own house - I recall when the movement was the model for struggle worldwide, I would the struggle once again be equated with the struggle for human dignity, my ultimate game is to represent the evolutionary impulse in humanity, that eternal urge to be greater than we are,

conduct yourself in a manner that does me
proud, live right, respect the mojo, and
you, too, can be the great hoodoo,

demoja

7ᵀᴴ MOVEMENT: DESTINYWORK
everyday I sit and play, the hoodoo board of destiny

7:43: hoodoo wordcraft
o queen mother morrison, be I worthy of the Craft

7:43:*1*: krik - the word - humanitys most powerful instrument, we communicate through the word, we respond to words, we define ourselves and our world through words, words cause people to act / do / be, each one an incantation, each one unto itself a work of art / spell and / or prayer, the word water cannot quench your thirst but the word mojo can feed your soul **- krak,**

7:43:*2*: when gathering folk around the sacred fire the telling itself is a blessing, transforming the writer in the writing, the reader in the reading, the listener in the moment, the teller in the tale - as the voice of a culture that has since its inception felt itself under siege, afroam lit is fundamentally shamanistic & vitally concerned with communal / cultural health and empowerment, creating the visions without which the people will perish and serving in its mythic heart its ageold griotic function of keeping the culture alive and viable, what we call *working in the tradition,*

7:43:*3*: in bambaraland initiates are called domas, the knowers, or donikebas, makers of knowledge - because they are intermediaries between this world and the spiritworld, the doma disciplines speech and does not utter it recklessly, a doma cannot tell a lie, but a griot is allowed to have two tongues - *there is no thing as important as the Work can be* - the power of narrative / nommo, a dogon word, the ability of words to forge new realities, the dinka masters of the fishing spear are defined by their power to make a thing so just be saying it is so, for masters of the fishing spear reality and the word must be in accord, for masters of the fishing spear words of power have influence only when they are true and pertinent, words of power must express what folk know to be true but are unable to articulate,

7:43:4: babajohn killens, the great griot master of brooklyn, considered the literary life a sacred calling and so do I - *be I worthy of the Craft* - conduct yourself as if you were in truth the great writer you aspire to be and you are, I once, in conversation with playwright, aishah rahman, said I wanted to be the greatest novelist ever lived, she said - *no art, thats not what you want, you want to sing your song the best you can sing it, that way you can appreciate other folk singing theirs,*

7:43:5: the way of the griot is a lifetime commitment to producing good, significant and beautiful works designed to evolve with time, wondrously multilinear works that grow with the interpretation of each generation, a force so immersed in the essence of the human condition that your every word is resonant with significance - *o life!* - said the druidic joyce - *I go to encounter for the millionth time the reality of experience and to forge in the smithy of my soul the uncreated conscience of my race,*

7:43:6: if you would Works that grow with time instead of being diminished by it you must grapple with issues humanity considers essential, issues humanity engages generation after generation, it is the responsibility of you who would be griot to be productive, significant & of the righteous, at all times willing to grow, to master your Craft, to work hard, to pay your dues without whimpering, creating works designed to finesse the human condition / the human spirit and / historical circumstance, timeless works so powerful they cannot be denied,

7:43:7: *there are times, fleeting moments,* when you being strong / disciplined / productive, or youve written a really good piece / passage / sentence, that you are acutely aware of yourself as historical / epochal / history in the flesh, there are moments when you have positioned yourself so precisely in the historical continuums center of balance that you are aware of being godforce / a focal point of reality and illusion / a nexus of generational possibility / conjuring reality into being through the sheer force of your will, your work, your craft and your game –

if you pull it off, you and your works will be studied and modeled in the hearts and aspirations of generations to come - to the extent that your works relevant and significant to those generations, to that extent are you immortal,

immortal

demoja

7:44: *hoodoo mythwork*
zora neale claim, my words true words,
my story true story, my lies true lies,

7:44:1: *mythwork, the primary tool of destinic guidance* and cultural custodianship, cultural narratives that tell the perceived story of a people, the cosmologies in which our lives find meaning, mythical fictions more real than real, it is mythwork that gives our lives purpose, it is mythwork that frame out our visions of who we are and aspire to be, it is mythwork that shapes our generations, our calls for collective action - it can be action appropriate to the historical movement, *reconstruction, the great migration, the civil rights movement*, or it can be catastrophically inappropriate, *a peoples temple, a xhosa cattlekilling,*

7:44:2: mythwork justifies cultural traits with supernatural authority, strong mythwork evolves as necessary to retain inspirational power, weak mythwork is mythwork you see through, your own cultures mythwork you just call reality, according to past master r.g.h. siu in **the craft of power,** a text that schooled me back in the day - *create a myth sustaining your movement like the deep ocean floating a majestic ship. draw an inspiring rationale for your past actions and present position, a ringing call for your continuing expansion, a vigorous condemnation of your formidable opposition, put your best minds on it,*

7:44:3: all Works are contemporary in creation, it is the mythological process, cultural value judgments, that determines which will be considered essential cultural phenomena / metastory / timeless / pertinent / even enjoyable / generations hence - the strongest vision will be the one most congruent with the great mojo,

7:44:4: true mythmaker is not subject to the myths of others, this what you do, this an illusion you see through, best mythwork always your own - you not a player if you not shaping your legacy, zora neales autobio more mythwork than truth, zora neale didnt have no respect for the truth, and for all his doing, nat love didnt became historical until he wrote his story down, a tenn slave who went west after the civil war and became a known character, deadwood dick, you seen that photo of him, aint you, long apache hair, pistol on his belt, boots, chaps, leaning on his rifle, classic black cowboy, but he was a elderly pullman porter when he wrote the memoir that made him historical - *mounted on my horse, my trusty lariat at hand and my guns on my belt I felt like I could defy the world, as I stop to ponder over the days of old, isnt it a wonder that some of us are alive to tell the tale,*

7:44:5: when the french finally captured macandal the slaves were commanded to watch their wanga man die at the stake, *where is his power now*, the french taunted, but when the flames were lit, macandal screamed and leapt from the pyre, the french swore they threw him back in but the slaves knew better & all that night conch horns echoed throughout the mountains - *macandal is free* - the conch should only be blown in times of greatest need, when survival of the tribe or its enslavement is at stake, hopefully you do not hear the haunting refrain of the conch in your lifetime but still you must know its power, the call of the conch must be instilled generation after generation through story and ritual so when the conch does call it stirs the soul – *it is a gathering of the tribes, bring shield, bring spear, battle has come to us,*

7:44:6: mythwork is often a destiny spell designed to counter or reinforce a prevailing worldview, I recall when menes united the two egypts and built his capital city of memphis, whereupon the memphite priests challenged the prevailing creation myth of the creator god, atum, creating through masturbation, by claiming their local god, ptah, created the world by thinking it, speaking it in a word, and then it was so - excellent mythwork, attuned to current political conditions & manifesting a higher plane, creative thought over masturbation, the divine over the animal, in the beginning was not the word but the thought,

The Hoodoo Book of Flowers

7:44:7: to bind mythology to a place is to make it holyground, sacred spaces to which divine narratives like this one have been attached - during the civil war the word went out to slaves in all 4 corners of the delta - *get to memphis and you free, the citadel on the bluff, the guardian at the gate – according to what I heard, 3 more times memphis will be found, a place, a star, a state of mind* - a hoodoo pilgrimage from the brooklyn grave of the babajohn, cemetery of the evergreens, beacon hill #2, #13358, proceeding through the doors of no return to rickydocs roost, radio host bob law once asked me - *how does it feel being part of the mythopoetic tradition of the delta* - question made my heart full, I try to represent, claim to be *the High Hoodoo of Memphis*, horse of the conqueror, pure mythwork, a title that tickle me - *call me I will come,*

7:44:8: returning culture hero mythwork strike me as the strongest move on the board, mean you transmutate as necessary, whatever the generations need, thats what you bringing - *I have been told that long as jebal barkal stands* the nubians cannot be defeated, I have been told it was the elders of jebal barkal called conch on the illuminated children of the sun, decreed they had to be scattered to the 4 corners of the earth and tempered in the holy hell of slavery for hoodoo missions and starflung destinies - I have been told jebal barkal still stands and the soul of galactic nubia rests in every heart

7:44:9: it was zora neale confabulated highjohn the conquer and the john the trickster slave tales into high john the conqueror as returning culture hero, article she wrote for the saturday evening post during WWII that took on a bonified life of its own, way zora neale told it the conqueror was a plant carried for protection, a root so strong it begin to walk and talk like a natural man, zora claim he helped free black folk from slavery by tricking ol massa, say once the slaves was free the conuqerors soul reside in de conqueror root to await the call whenever blackfolk in need, zora say whenever you in trouble you just whisper his name and you will feel him in the breeze, whispering in the trees, zora say he the burdenbearer, the hopebringer, the battlefighter, the jackpotwinner, zora say when you need him you call him and he will be there before you get the words out your mouth, highjohn the conqueror, the mighty conqueroo,

thats what zora neale say, ask her yourself if you dont believe me,

demoja

7:45: the hoodoo way
come papa labas, come open this gate, in the name of the conqueror, let this work be done

7:45:1: de hoodoo way is de indigenous african american spiritual tradition, one of a family of afrospiritual traditions in the americas, vodou / lucumi / candomble / obeah / et al / religions mostly, fusions of catholicism and various african systems, yoruba / fon / congo / et al / whereas hoodoo has traditionally been a congofused folkmagic system, folk hear hoodoo they generally thinking folkmagic hoodoo, slaverytime hoodoo, 100 years out of date hoodoo, spells, hells, and black cat bones, a cultural curiosity, evil perhaps, foolish at best, a halloween clown show,

The Hoodoo Book of Flowers

7:45:2: hoodoo been high damn near a 100 years now, mama whodun say the hoodoo the appropriators do is the hoodoo they have read about but by the time its written down we have already moved on, *this is a living tradition*, she say, a custodial tradition root deep, custodial hoodoo is defined in context of the community for which you accept responsibility, the comforters of ras hui I, healing affliction,

7:45:3: the moral laws of the universe are pretty consistent across the great traditions, a great way engages the questions for which there are no answers, a great way teaches you to live in the spirit, to nurture your soul through service, a great way transcends the primacy of survival & the constraints of reality, a great way doesnt promise a life of ease, it promises the strength to deal with affliction, equanimity in the face of struggle, a great way is a door to the cosmic divine, a crossroads - to be a great way you have to universalize your tribal licks,

7:45:4: among the dogon of mali, the hogon is master of the cosmic seed, every aspect of the hogons life unites the hogon to the cosmic order, the hogons sandals are the ark of nommo, the colors of the hogons tunic represent the 4 corners of the earth, the hogons spiral headdress reflects the path of the cosmic seed, the hogons house is a model of the universe, to the right of the door is the hogons staff, the axis of the world, to the left is the pouch of the world, in the dry season their positions are reversed, the 8 steps of the hogons porch represent the 1st 8 chiefs of the dogon, in the morning the hogon faces east for blessings, in the evening the west - in every particular the hogons day expresses participation in cosmic harmony and by his movements controls the cosmic cycles, the personification of the universe,

7:45:5: study many traditions, determine what works for you and extract the best they have to give, walk any path and swim in the great mojo - de cross & de crescent, de star & de bodhi tree, de tao & de om, de yoruba, de fon & de congo, de haitians, de brazilians & de cubans, too, de hoodoo way encompass them all, take up the best they have to give and forge your own, like ras sewell say - *live a royal life, that others may admire you, dont live the same level as your opponents and your adversaries. I show you de fullness of rasta, what is written in de bible, rasta live above dat,*

7:45:6: anymethod anytime is what hyatt called the hoodoo principle in his 5 vol. oral history compendium, *hoodoo, conjuration, witchcraft & rootwork*, one of the core texts of hoodoo, *anymethod anytime* refer to hoodoos affinity for breaking the laws of magic as called for, any Work you do there is more than one way to do it and no two practitioners Work the same, hoodoo lost more of its african nature than the other afrospiritual traditions of the americas, the bastard tradition of a bastard culture it is accretive, adapting the best of everything it touches, a cultural flexibility conferring potential advantage in an evolving oneworld reality

7:45:7: I surmise if a culture is dysfunctional its the fault of its indigenous spiritual system, if vodou was doing its job haiti wouldnt be in the shape its in, same same hoodoo, it is because of this I would forge of the hoodoo way an instrument of spiritual and political redemption, an african american way, guide and guardian of human destiny, the magical negro wrote large in de geas of rickydoc - *half my family give consultations,* my mama once told me, *other half wont make a move without one,*

awaken the sleeper,
protect the weak,
guide the strong,

The Hoodoo Book of Flowers

demoja

7:46: hoodoo magic
come wanganegresse, queenmother magic, come make it real

7:46:1: hoodoo magic has traditionally been folk magic,
but the cutting edge has long since moved into high magic –

*the enhancement of the human condition
and the amelioration of suffering /
playing with reality and the potentially divine human mind /
shaping reality / shaping generations / spiritdoctoring /
making real into the world that which was not /
oneness with the universal divine /*

civilians never quite know what to do with magic and magicians, is it real or is it a trick / an illusion / yet high magicians have been a part of every society ever been, shrouded deep in the mystery that is part and parcel of our power,

7:46:2: 1ˢᵗ step in magic is the decision to step on the path magical, convincing yourself that you are in truth the great magician you aspire to be, in order to conjure you must believe, the way other folk believe in god you must believe in yourself, in your meditations remove all doubt, letting a mantra of magical empowerment sink deeper and deeper into your consciousness - *my magic is powerful, my will is law* - adopt a magical name represent the mythical you, keep your magical self secret until your power can withstand realitys scorn, until you are capable of being a viable counterreality, step up too soon and reality will deny you, raptors will pick your bones,

7:46:3: magical meditation is the ability to create mental images and feed them, investing mojo until they are real in the world, study the texts, subject your magical theories to ruthless testing until you understand the logic of it, magic must make sense to your scholarly nature, apply experimental principles to the pursuit of it, the high magician is primarily a scholar whose power is based on mission critical knowledge, the true magician strives to stay contemporary with the advance of knowledge about the nature of the world, going a step further - *experimenting with the further reaches of the potentially divine human mind, a conjunctive state of mind / will / way that enables the aspiring magician to utilize timeproven magical / ideological technology to shape the destiny of humanity and the fabric of reality - to conjure, if you will, grandmaster of time, space & being,*

7:46:4: the most fundamental magic is word magic, words are compulsive, words create new realities, forge new visions through nommo, the power to speak reality and then it is so

7:46:5: never depend on magic to do what only action can, magic is a supplement to action, not a replacement, marie leveau may have had direct contact with the spirits but it was her spy system of domestics that delivered the secrets of the powerful, magic is too often the cargo cult refuge of the powerless, always try mundane measures first - high haint fred douglass, a known trouble maker, was hired out to edward covey, known slave breaker, who commence right away to breaking him, one day another slave gave baba douglass a root he said would stop the beatings but the beatings continued until the day douglass snatched up a limb and beat that man so severe he never raised a hand to him again, his high john root gave him confidence to defy his master, to conquer his fear, magic is best used for attitude adjustment, whatever the call, in all things magical one asks the blessings of wanganegresse, an offering of magical memphis medicinal tea, homebrew, will bring the magic of wanganegresse to your aid in any condition,

7:46:6: *it is legba, in his incessant quest for knowledge*, once again attempt to calibrate the cosmos, once again god deny this attempt at godhead, your knowledge, said mawu-lisa, is still not sufficient, this when legba invent high magic, what is this new thing, the people ask, legba reply that this is high magic, making real into the world that which was not, you are no longer slaves of the gods - this when mawu-lisa, no longer amused, make legba invisible so he can no longer be human but must always be vodoun, the one trick the shapeshifting lord of the crossroads can no longer pull, now whenever harm come to humanity god blames legba - *I have put their well being in your care, you must do better,*

7:46:7: *in your hoodoo maturity reach for power in the world,* influencing the influents, consultant to the powerful, a power in the arena *(guide the strong)* - then look at you in your eldership, an armchair revolutionary securely encased in an anansic web of power forged during your days in the field, what good theories that have not been tempered in the arena,

shapeshifters at play, guide and
guardian of the hoodoo way,

demoja

7:47: hoodoo conjuration
grandmaster snake 2g, o lord of the
changes, work this reality to my liking

7:47:1: conduct yourself as you aspire to be and you are, this is the essence of conjuration, to conjure you 1st forge the desired reality in your mind and then you hold onto it until reality adjusts itself to your will, Ima tell it to you like uncle tom williams, past master of the hoodoo way, when asked if he could handle a case, replied, *son, I can do most anything,*

7:47:2: the commencement of any work is its formulation, that which is to be manifested must 1st be conceived, if you believe a thing is so, you take steps to make it so, the competent hoodoo adept is a realityplayer skilled in the creation and vitalization of magical imagery, reality is much more fluid than most folk realize, an ever evolving consensus of perception, every second of existence one of infinite possibility, its options activated by choice - *crossroads work,*

7:47:3: doc english (hcw&r): *I have been so good I could take a glass of water and make anything appear in it,*

7:47:4: its relatively easy to conjure your own reality, its conjuring other folks reality make you a master,

7:47:5: first you must convince them of your power, then offer them a vision that inspires them to their very best Fa, take them to the crossroads - if your conjuration is strong enough it supersedes the reality of others, same same art, you create the vision in your mind, you pour everything you got into it until its real in the world, a song, a book, a spell, a painting, baba snake 2G gibbs speculating physics on a bass guitar,

The Hoodoo Book of Flowers

conjurations come easier if snake 2G providing the soundtrack, anything bass, anything deep,

7:47:6: aligned with the laws of nature and buttressed through human will & imagination, anything is possible, it should be understood, however, that in duels of this nature reality generally wins, moving reality is more than a notion but if you move reality even just a little bit it changes things, most folk live in the material world with only glimpses of the spiritual, the conjuror is a two head individual what lives with a head in both worlds, free of realitys constraints - dont waste all that power, when you make your move make it rootwork strong, crossroads strong,

7:47:7: when playing with reality there are certain laws you just cannot violate, you can leap off a cliff if you want but based on our current knowledge base you cannot expect to fly, the best magic is good common sense, but reality is much more fluid than most folk realize, it, too, is a conjuration - it was amma of mali's dogon created the 266 signs that embrace all things, the first creation of the world was a failure, ogo defied her and tried to create his own universe but was unable to say the words which would bring the universe into being, he was unable to wield nommo, the sacred words that create, he knew not the hoodoo word of creation - *demoja*,

7:47:8: black culture is predisposed to respect conjure, blackfolk still believe in hoodoo, dont care what they say, they want and need to believe their tribal medicine folk still got the magic, still got the power, when they realize Im trying to retool hoodoo for a 21st century sensibility, forge of it an instrument of spiritual and political redemption, they willing to listen, they are in fact eager for me to be real, a brand new kind of hoodooman, east africa they call me mganga maua, medicine man flowers, woman once stop me in the street, say your book saved my life - *wanted a nobel but I will take what I can get,*

7:47:9: estevanico the moor crossed the united states as a slave on the narvaez expedition, one of 80 survivors of a storm that stranded them in florida, whittled down to 4 over the years they spent crossing the continent, often as slaves of various tribes, from one such master they learned the medicine man trade and as medicinemen they traveled across the west healing folk, led by the most exotic one, the black one, adorned in feathers, furs and turquoise, followed everywhere by 100s of believers until repatriated by a column of conquistadors - couple of years later, estevan, still a slave, was forced by the governor of mexico to scout for an expedition looking for the 7 cities of gold, and became, once again, chakwaina, kachina rain maker, once again adorned in fetishes, furs, feathers, and followers, leaving a trail of crosses to guide the spanish forces behind him until at the zuni village of kawikuh he disappears from the historical record, reputedly killed when the zuni reject his claim - when the spanish are told about the death of their scout they retreat under the watchful eye of chakwaina, finally free,

when you one with the great mojo even
reality must yield to the hoodoo will

demoja

7:48: hoodoo prophecy
such is my luck, such I have been called to see, and let it come rough or smooth, I must surely bear it

7:48:1: every tradition has a system of renewal and regeneration, the prophetic impulse, specially designated spiritual workers operating outside of priestly hierarchies and vested interests, considered divinely guided to reform / renew / regenerate stagnant traditions / offer new & improved understanding of god - folk think prophecy is about foretelling the future, au contrary, prophecy is correlating current behavior with destinic consequence - *continue to conduct yourselves in this manner and your generations will suffer, listen to me and they will flourish, god told me this, divinity bid me sing,*

7:48:2: if you would be anointed a prophetic voice by your culture, you must 1st prove yourself through selfless service, the stakes are much too high for it to be easy to claim prophet, there is no curse quite like that of an uninformed prophet, much less a venal one - true prophet must be able to bear the crippling responsibility that come with the power to shape human destiny, when once to save a people he condemned another, the babajohn, asked who was he to judge, replied who else would I trust with measures of this magnitude,

7:48:3: most folk claim prophet trying to trick you, any spiritual worker ask you for your money / labor / life / love / soul is a demon to be cast out of your world with the quickness - *what were those jonestown folk thinking, you wonder* - if it dont make sense to you, reject it, Im told the long juju oracle of dahomey supported its priests through enslavement of unlucky supplicants, what kind of hoodoo is that, no cattlekilling for me, thank you, reject it,

7:48:4: resist the hunger for credit and validation, among the doma, the knowers, the spiritual masters of mali, a doma grand master is not afraid of the unfavorable opinion of various

The Hoodoo Book of Flowers

publics, willing to accept scorn / indifference / embarrassment, countering any and all disrespect with relentless dignity / service / mojo, error is publicly acknowledged as obligation, purification from defilement,

7:48:5: rembe of the lugbara, claiming to be a horse of adro, used the yakan water cult to gather enough lugbara to defy the germans under emin pasha, when he was defeated one of his captured warriors was asked why did you follow a man whose charms you never believed would keep you safe from bullets - *we did not know the belgians and feared them,* he replied, *rembe came to show us that the europeans were people, he showed us how to fight the belgians and not fear them and their strength, you do not abandon a leader who has given his all in his time of greatest need,*

*7:48:6: one day ngendeng, a leopard skin priest of the nue*r, announced himself the voice of dengkur, for months he lived alone in the bush, separating himself, as must any wouldbe prophet, from his society in order to gain control of it, when ngendeng finally called a gathering of spears to resist arab slavers who had been reaping slaves with impunity, he had prepared them using the prophetic codes of nuer culture, witness the testimony of nat the prophet - *having soon discovered to be great, I must appear so, and therefore studiously avoided mixing in society, and wrapped myself in mystery, devoting my time to fasting and prayer,*

7:48:7: when martin met his destiny at the lorraine motel it solidified his mythwork and finessed his death, the ancestors welcoming him into the ancestral fold, ancestorship is not automatic, it must be maintained through ritual and remembrance, through the immortal witness of stories, long as you remembered and ritualed your traveling spirit still out there taking care of business, imagine, if you will, that dark and stormy night at the temple when martin spoke in tongues - *well I dont know what will happen now, we've got some difficult days ahead, but it really doesnt matter with me now, because Ive been to the mountaintop and I dont mind, like anybody I would like to live a long life, longevity has its place but Im not concerned about that now, I just want to do gods will, and hes allowed me to go to the mountain, and Ive seen the promised land, I might not get there with you, but I want you to know tonight, that we as a people will get to the promiseland,*

7:48:8: a gathering of the gods is called to order, an unruly congregation of hoary old certainties, vigorous new upstarts, and elder gods fading into myth, legend and academe, usually a gathering of this sort engender a kind of divine tension but this matter concerns them all, this new prophet has become a problem, thats the nature of these wouldbe prophets, grumble one of the elder gods. more trouble than they worth, I hear he claim to represent an africanamerican pantheon, proclaim an ancient deity known to be particularly good at all hearing, this provoke a round of divine laughter and much needed tension relief, what, pray tell, is an africanamerican pantheon, what on earth could that be, well, say an upstart divinity, funny as that might be to yall, I believe this newcomer just might be the real thing. I foresee changes in the order of things - this sober the assemblage. the gods truly do not like change, they generally prefer things stay as they are, forever, suspicion fall upon the gods of africa, some of his licks appear mighty familiar, what do you folk know of this matter. the gods of africa profess ignorance but legba appear to be speaking out both sides of his mouth and oshun is blushing, I do believe, they say, rickydoc is in the house,

The Hoodoo Book of Flowers

7:48:9: the wouldbe prophet manifests through works designed to interact synergistically with the human condition, the human spirit and historical circumstance, works designed to evolve through time instead of being decimated by it, if your prophetic tradition is respected by the tribe you are given the dispensation (having proved yourself worthy) to break old traditions and forge new ones - I claim prophetic dispensation to position hoodoo as the prophetic tradition of the afrospiritual world and all humanity - *trying to mack myself into the game* - positioning african american culture as one of the influential cultures of the future, positing a race of players with a vision of themselves as a people of power and purpose,

cast your vision, young hoodoo, as far as you can see, determine the challenges the tribe will face, prepare the tribal soul to meet them,

de mo ja

7:49: hoodoo destinywork
o come babajohn, grandmaster of the longgame, come come show me the way

7:49:1: every high hoodoo should have a strategy of empowerment, a hoodoo mission, a mix of tactical initiatives in play at any given time, longgame shaping generations on the hoodoo board of destiny, the arena upon which we are all players and played, every body, every institution, all pieces to be placed as you see fit, everybody is in play on the hoodoo board of destiny, including you,

7:49:2: ideological orchestrations: monitoring destinic dynamics and positioning your vision to be the most important vision shaping human destiny at this historical point and time, a necessary delusion for masterwork on the board, like magic you got to believe it before you can claim ideological orchestrator, destiny players with competing visions / narratives of reality, each trying to ensure their vision is the one future generations live by, master players who count game in generations, past masters of the crossroads, adept in the orchestration of belief systems - I once read somewhere it takes 3 generations minimal to program a new headset, what we know in our minds, our children will know in their hearts, our grandchildren in their souls,

7:49:3: according to the iching there are two ways for the superior personality to influence the world, either at court influencing the influents, or in withdrawal from the world to work on yourself as a model of what is to come, I translate that as a cycle of engagement & withdrawal, some secrets expose themselves only to the solitude of the sage, but what good are theories that have not been tempered in the arena.

7:49:4: as hoodoo adepts, trained cultural forces and ideological orchestrators, you will leave a legacy by definition, your presence on the planet will matter, you dont get to choose that, what you do get to choose is what that legacy will be, what do you want folk to think / feel / do / be when they think of you, what do you want your name to stand for,

7:49:5: I was on a greyhound bus to LA, flatbroke and busted, fleeing heartbreak and cocaine, my belief in myself and my power shattered, my dark night of the soul, who I was / had been no longer worked, I did not realize how desperate my need until around oklahoma I came upon a watchtower pamphlet (free reading material) that discussed the nature of a good holybook and / or tradition, said a new tradition (obviously referring to their own) that wanted to compete with established traditions had to prove itself by its works - *had to be a true advance in human understanding and empowerment / had to promote truly universal fellowship instead of just that of the believer / had to provide a realistic 21st century alternative to established traditions / one closer to the truth of things / had to enable a moral, ethical life, one of wisdom and understanding / had to be a tolerant, loving way / asking the very best of its adherents / had to be an evolved understanding wrapped up in an appealing mythology / said the true test of a good, healthy spiritual tradition is that its adherents lead good, healthy lives / brimming with strength & meaning, beauty & grace / that they build strong, healthy communities / asked do its believers benefit / does it provide a coherent all-encompassing worldview / is it a cosmology by which its believers can understand and manifest the meaning and purpose of life / asked what laws does it set forth to regulate human life and living / are these laws of life as consistent and fundamental as gravity, / does it inspire its believers in the struggle and challenges of life / does it provide in times of need / does it comfort in times of despair / does it renew the weary and guide the strong / does it nourish the spirit / does it celebrate life / are its believers healthy, wealthy and wise, strong and enlightened, productive and respected / do they live lives rich in contentment, achievement and significance / does it give its believers power in the world / power in the spirit / the power to master the flesh and the baser nature / the power to triumph over evil, within and without / does it give them the power to tap their fullest human potential / to make them godlike / does it deliver unto its believers a miracle working power / are they a beautiful people / are they blessed / is it an open gate, o traveler, a point of contact with*

The Hoodoo Book of Flowers

the divine / the supreme power of the universe / the great mojo in its many names and infinite manifestations -

same same, it said, about a wouldbe holybook, wouldnt it be nice, I thought, to write a text did all that, and just like that, I had my mojo back,

7:49:6: I look at the condition of the black people and wherever we are in the world we are on the bottom of our respective societies, everywhere, cant blame everywhere on nobody but ourselves, somehow someway we must transform into strengths the weaknesses that have crippled us in global competition - we've tried every strategy there is, all to no avail, we still americas bottomfeeders, I have concluded that as long as we a weakminded people nothing will work, I got to transform blackfolk souldeep, shape my generations into the people I would have them be, I am a spiritdoctor after all, souls is what I do,

7:49:7: ever since I can remember I have wanted to be a hero, a champion of the race, too many comics in my developmental years I guess, I dont have to be super, I just want to be a hero, one of humanitys great teachers, I want the generations to love me - when I claim geas by rickydoc Im claiming prophetic dispensation to forge new ways, hoping that through a life of selfless service, through the power of my nommo and the quality of my analysis, the culture will eventually anoint me as a cultural custodian worth listening to, a prophet of the hoodoo way, I, too, have had a vision:

7:49:8: the daylight dream of rickydoc: *I see a culture respected throughout the galaxy, guide and guardian of human destiny, of our ongoing struggle to evolve, to be greater than we are - I ask only that you be the great and glorious people*

you were meant to be, the illuminated children of the sun, humanitys living ancestors, gods true chosen,

7:49:9: I figure the best use of my brief time on the planet and my particular skillset is to do an african american holybook, found an african american way, I figure a good holybook shape many generations, hopefully even a middling one will do, ultimately I want to represent the evolutionary impulse in humanity, that eternal urge to be greater than we are, the eternal responsibility to reach for the next step in humanitys ongoing quest to be - what I call destinywork,

I ask guidance, not for myself but those for whom I bear responsibility, that I might be worthy

demoja

8ᵀᴴ MOVEMENT: ILLUMINATION
in a world of illusion, let me see true

8:50: hoodoo wisdom
queenmother dorisjean, cool
mama wisdom, come to me

8:50:1: *from experience comes knowledge,* from knowledge wisdom, examine every thing for wisdom value, the difference between knowledge and wisdom is knowing whats essential and whats peripheral, it is a trained instinct to the significant, dare to be wise,

8:50:2: *wisdom presuppose a certain equanimity* untouched by turbulence, a certain generosity of spirit / a certain knowledge base to draw upon / a functional knowledge of the world and different cultures / a certain dignity in all things – wisdom presuppose an obsession with what it means to live a good life, ital life, wisdom presuppose the regulation of emotional and ethical conduct / and, I furthermore believe it presuppose a lasting contribution to the enhancement of the human condition and the alleviation of human misery - wisdom is, I surmise, a function of maturity, no matter what stage of life you want to be mature for your age, you want to be wise,

8:50:3: *to achieve wisdom* you must couple scholarship with life experience and contextual flexibility, what might be wisdom today might not be wisdom tomorrow, what might be wisdom here might not be wisdom there, wisdom never rest – dont be like me, so many years I aspired to be wise, when I finally achieved wisdom I gave it all over to pride,

8:50:4: back in the day man and woman was equal in all regard when one day man decide he want to rule, so he go find god lounging around in paradise and ask if he can have strength to rule over all things - including woman, god ask dubiously, specially woman, say man - god not sure this gon work but he give man a heaping helping of strength and send him on his way, fore you know it man ruling everything, naming the animals and all, claiming shit, paying low taxes, sitting pretty, when woman come home that evening he say he is in charge now, cause god give me all the strength, I am the boss, but dont you worry none, little darling, Ima be a benevolent boss cause you cool with me - woman dont appreciate this not one bit so she go to paradise and she ask god to give her strength enough to match mans and god say, sorry, I cant do that, what I give I dont take back, thats when woman notice a sack of wisdom over in the corner and say well can I have that there sack of wisdom then, god say what you gon do with all that wisdom, I gotta warn you, that wisdom more trouble than its worth, thats why Im throwing it out, woman say dont you worry none about that, god, just give me that wisdom there and we gon call it square, and so it come to pass that woman and man was equals again, more or less,

8:50:5: a rich man once asked the babajohn if he could buy some wisdom and the babajohn said, was I to sell it you couldnt afford it, you must do as I do and serve humanity until wisdom finds you,

8:50:6: lord god nyame often task anansi with matters of great importance, this show god has a sense of humor, so it come to pass that soon after nyame begin the world the new humans were struggling, taking too long to figure things out, so nyame brew up a strong batch of wisdom and entrust it to anansi - *look here anansi, want you to spread this here wisdom around so everybody get a helping, so they know how to live life ital* - but anansi decide to keep all the wisdom himself, so he start weaving a web to hide his new wisdom stash in the great baobab bottletree but he trying to climb the great baobab, weave the web, and hold onto the wisdom pot at the same time, and even anansi dont have hands enough for all that, about halfway up the sunlight off those bottles confuse him and the pot slip from his fingers and when that pot of wisdom hit the ground it break open so hard little pieces of wisdom fly all over the world, so much wisdom anybody want some can get some, just you got to work for it now, and all you gon get is just a little bitty helping cause thats all thats out there now, but when it come to wisdom thats all you need, just enough to make a way,

8:50:7: *wisdom is a process,* no one is born wise, aspire ye to wisdom and walk in grace for all your days, a traveler who knows the road, an old soul,

this text is a wisdom spell, generating mojo every time it is read, transforming the world,

demoja

8:51: *hoodoo compassion*
let me walk in the compassion of o killens wherein all blessings are found

8:51:1: *it is compassion that ensures our survival as a species,* it is compassion provides for the social contract that understands we are no more than the least of us, it is compassion that gives us the ability to look past self and prioritize others / caring for folk outside your circle as you do for the folk inside it / expanding your consciousness vs constraining it / attaining cosmic vs tribal consciousness / assuming responsibility for all jah creature, great and small / understanding that to alleviate the suffering of others is to alleviate my own,

8:51:2: it is increasingly difficult to insulate ourselves from the tribulations of those less fortunate, we are all, it appears, in this together, the mystics, the great teachers, have always known this but growing globalization has made us all mystics and teachers, we are, the least of us, able to experience other cultures, other voices, other ways, in a manner unprecedented, we are, all of us, notes in the great song - make a stranger smile, I dare you, 2 strangers, double dare you,

8:51:3: compassion that does not manifest in the world is a waste of compassion, whats the point if not deployed, deployed but not displayed, compassion as theater is corruptive, and do remember this, young conjure, when taking burdens off broken shoulders, transferring them to your sturdy own, be careful of burnout, that dont help nobody, know how to say no,

8:51:4: there are folk with whom we feel a connection, for whom it is easy to feel compassion, but what about folk who make us uneasy, folk who are different, folk we dont understand, much less folk who evil and unsavory, folk who do not deserve our empathy, but the compassion of o killens should not dependent on worth, if you are compassionate only to the deserving how then are you of the elect, finesse those who mean you harm with unadulterated hoodoo blessings, shower them all with the compassion of o killens - now this dont mean you run around town with your guard down, sitting with your back to the door and getting played, means you always put a little compassion in the mix, a lot of compassion when you can,

8:51:5: in my youth I aspired to be a hard man with a hard plan, game then was to forge blackfolk into a conquering horde and fling them into battle, power was my constant study and pursuit, this was reflected in my work and my character, one day the babajohn pulled me aside and said - *art, you a brilliant writer but with a little compassion you could be profound* - all I heard was brilliant, wasnt till many years later, after life had humbled me some, that I understood what the babajohn was trying to tell me, trying to make sure my contribution, as his student, would not be hard and cold but warm and loving, an old shaman trying to ensure the health of the tribal soul,

8:51:6: I have a conflict I have been unable to resolve, do I speak for black people, or do I speak for all humanity, all humanity is the strong move but I cant leave black people defenseless, unable to resolve this fundamental conflict, I have tried to Work with both hands, represent both my families, blackfolk and all humanity, universalize my tribal imperatives, I understand now what all truly effective black leaders come to see, cant just save my own, got to save them all,

8:51:7: I understand now that the high hoodoo without compassion is a rogue force, that power without compassion is a sin, it is the compassion of o killens inform everything I do,

supreme good fortune,

demoja

8:52: hoodoo meditation
come ra khu, o guardian of da cosmic spaces, open this door

8:52:1: meditation: attuning yourself to the world within / without, fine tuning the mind / soul, gaining control of your thoughts / your self / world / cosmos / godhead - meditation focuses the mind and calms the soul, makes your life magical / cosmic / godlike - the mind is a powerful instrument, specially for travelers like us, it must be made to understand it is a servant, not a master,

8:52:2: study different systems in order to develop your own, using the best of what works for you, the 1st step meditational is to sit . . . still . . . this posture should be natural, effortless, avoid exotic positions unnatural to your culture, the royal seat is upright, hands on your knees, comfortable spread, royal presentation – *morning? night? how long? eyes open? eyes closed? music? no music? which music?* quien sabe, experiment, experiment, experiment - try many systems, try many techniques to determine what works best for you, continue to refine it, evolve it, make it learn new tricks,

8:52:3: basic meditation routine: sit comfortably but alert in a chosen spot thats sacred to you, or at least private, quiet, your personal altarspace, where you can be you, adorn your altar with icons of power, fetishes that make you feel good and strong, not just good, not just strong, good and strong, settle yourself, attend to your breathing, access the great mojo within / without, center yourself in the beating heart of the universe and gain control of your unruly mind - *a mojo band could be helpful here* - access trancestates through mantras / disciplines / prayers / spells designed to address your needs,

8:52:4: the mind will drift, do not freak, it is the nature of human consciousness to drift, gently nudge it back into the desired state, human thought is sequential, become conscious of the stream, slow it down, control it, discipline it, sequence it in a problem solving manner, you cant control random thoughts but you can control the amount of attention they get, become aware of awareness, the unleashed mind flits from flower to flower, the mental default is action, even in stillness the mind is still racing, slow it down, step back and observe it, just ob serve it, slow it down,

8:52:5: *de meditational disciplines:*
deep meditations - for soothing the soul & enhancing the day
magical meditations - through realization of magical imagery
occult meditations - paranormal experimentation
healing meditations -physical / spiritual health & healing
destinic meditations - boardwork, cosmological exploration
centering meditations - godhead

8:52:6: *de mundane disciplines:* focus / clarity / stress reduction / awareness / consciousness / serenity / peace of mind / enhanced perceptual clarity / & quality of life / better, more conscious life choices / godhead,

de occult disciplines: de traveling spirit / altered states / visions / sensory experiences / occult powers - *distractions / distractions / nothing but distraction, do not tarry, do not get off the train,*

de walking disciplines: bringing the spiritual into your daily grind / being mindful whatever you do / operational consciousness / the hoodoo blink / serenity 2.0 / spiritvision on command / godhead,

de spiritual disciplines: insight / illumination / wisdom / generosity of spirit / serenity 3.0 / divine consciousness / godhead / grace,

8:52:7: align your internal dialogues with your goals and dreams, your brain talks to itself all the time, folk use to interpret this dialogue as the voice of god / demons / et al, but we know now the bicameral mind is in constant dialogue, control it, use it, sequence it - the human brain is designed to consider all options, including those you determine to be unacceptable to your soulwork - *master the withering death* - severing emotional attachment with unacceptable thoughts by calmly and patiently withdrawing allegiance until offending thoughts come less and less with less and less energy - *withering away* - fill that emptied space with mantras training you to whatever you need to be, bring your conduct into alignment with your rootwork and you good to go,

8:52:8: program de hoodoo blink, one blink and you in a spirit mode / a hoodoo state of mind / the spiritvision that see through illusion / capable of modality / deepening situational awareness and life experience / empowering the ability to finesse pain and confusion at will / the ability to effect serenity in the eye of the storm / instant attitude adjustment - I once heard of an adept, when told to meditate on silence, returned to the babajohn complaining that a bird had disturbed his silence, to which the babajohn reply, your practice cant be very strong if it cant handle the song of a fucking bird,

8:52:9: the cosmic disciplines: in magical meditation the goal is not the subconscious but the supraconsciousness / the universal consciousness / giving yourself over to the cosmic embrace of Fa / the godhead / the supreme serenity of divinity,

I am one with the great mojo,
de mo ja de mo ja de mo ja

8:53: hoodoo illumination
come mama day, come light my way,
in the name of papa CE I see

8:53:1: illumination: to bring light into the darkness / clarity and understanding to confusion / to see through illusion and deception / the ability to see past the surface to the essence of things / to perceive patterns unseen / to see the hammer before the hammer see you - applying spiritvision focuses the moment on whats truly significant,

8:53:2: how can you believe anything you have not questioned, beliefs you were given and have not earned, the first step of illumination is to free yourself from the mythology of your own culture, only then can you truly see, only then can you be truly free, hoodoo autonomy is to be aware of forces that manipulate you, advertising / retoric / religious, familial and social expectation / books like this one - when the babajohn got to heaven he was told to knock on the gate but he hesitated, how, he said, do I know this is not an illusion, and with that the gates of heaven opened, welcoming one of their own.

8:53:3: back when the world was still young brer rabbit and brer bear was disputing who the best, brer rabbit say look at these ears, friend, I hear most better than anybody, see that hill over there, I hear bees buzzing a honey tree and I can tell by the buzz that the honey is sweet, well, say brer bear, I acknowledge your hearing but how well can you smell, in that very same tree there is a nest, in that nest I smell two eggs and I can tell the far hand egg is a wee bit stale - so they still disputing who best when they hear a sound below and see little sister ground hog at her front door, and she say fellas, I cant do my chores for all this commotion at my door, lets run a little test to see who best on this hill, I acknowledge you can smell and hear better than most but tell me how well can you see, then she cut the horizon with a mighty gaze that wander all about the world and out amongst the stars till she say I have seen enough, I have looked high and I have looked low, seen all thats been and will ever be, and all I see are two of the biggest fools that ever could be, aint got nothing better to do than argue about who better than who,

8:53:4: when giving hard truths ask yourself, is it true, is it kind, is it compassionate, is it essential, is it necessary, is it good, learn to express truths that do not threaten those in need of it - newly freed from slavery the great greek storyteller, aesop the ethiop, decided to visit the delphic oracle, expecting to find wisdom he found only pride and greed, *curiosity brought me here,* he told them, *but what at a distance appears a mighty edifice upon arrival is naught but a pile of garbage* - afraid he would trash the brand, the citizens of delphi accused him of stealing a gold cup from the temple and threw him off the edge of a cliff, before he died he told them the story of a traveler with 2 donkeys, one to ride, the other to carry his goods, beset with a storm that spooked his donkeys they fell over a precipice, upon which the traveler lament his fate, *thrown off a cliff by jackasses,*

8:53:5: did I ever tell you about the time queenmother memphis come upon truth clad in rags, damn near naked, empty beggar bowl in hand, she say truth you looking a little peaked these days and truth say times been hard, folk dont respect me like they use to, well no wonder, say the queen mother, look at you, sweetie, aint you had no home training - so queenmother memphis wash truth and groom truth and dress truth up in some fetching metaphor, drape some lyrical touches here and there, before you know it truth looking pretty good, doing pretty good in the marketplace, too - naked truth put anybody off their feed,

8:53:6: the hoodoo blink activates the spiritvision that sees beyond illusion, that exposes the spirit of things - to be hoodoo blind is to live in illusion, anything thats not of the spirit is illusion, if its not essential its a distraction - soul fevers like *hate / insecurity / pettiness / jealousy / envy / anger / rage / et all /* nothing but distractions, therefore illusion, focusing on anything thats not truly significant, anything that does not engage the spirit, it is the ongoing quest for significance that prioritize the eternal over the transient - when true vision is critical, when you need to dispel illusion, I suggest calling on babarod jackman, a hoodoo blink will suffice, being caught up in illusion is shedding mojo,

8:53:7: all revelation aint revelation, when you play with reality sometime reality win, the human mind can convince itself of anything, judge a mystical experience by its fruits, by the health of your interpretation, if your interp is not healthy, reject it, you know when your soul has been stained, reject it, truth revealed is the philosophers stone, dispelling illusion, revealing whats real, I dont care how pleasant it appear, if it aint real reject it -

8:53:8: every moment in life is one of choice, how well you spend it depends on how well you see, on your sense of the significant, for those who see a sign will suffice, for those who do not no explanation will do - its not the number of experiences but the quality of what you get from them, your sense of the significant is what determines value to your soulwork - thats what nyamoy would tell you, she who brews beer in the market place where the heroes gather, in payment she gathers the myths and tales that gather when heroes do and weaves them into a tapestry that shows the truths that lie hidden beneath the legends, all who see it are struck blind, unless of course you too are a hero, in which case you will see your Fa,

8:53:9: testimony by mama day - *the island got spit out from the mouth of god, and when it fell to the earth it brought along an army of stars. He tried to reach down and scoop them back up, and found Himself shaking hands with the greatest conjure woman on earth. 'leave 'em here, lord,' she said, 'I aint got nothing but these poor black hands to guide my people, but I can lead on with light.'*

there is no need to call on the conqueror,
the conqueror has called on you,

demoja

8:54: hoodoo cleansing
big mama shepherdqueen, sanctify me
cleanse me, make me whole again,

8:54:1: hoodoo cleansings, the removal of impurities must precede any Working, magical or spiritual, the instruments must be purified and none more so than your own, it behoove you to cleanse the soul as regularly as you do the body, a disposition to holiness that must be won again and again, do not allow error to take root in your edifice, ruthlessly and continuously cast out all that is inferior if you would be a superior soul, sanctify yourself,

The Hoodoo Book of Flowers

8:54:2: the true nature of alchemy lies in purifying the dross of experience to extract its spiritual value, prioritizing the spiritual over the physical, the real over the apparent - goober dust blessings that sanctify and illuminate any condition, for the haters love, for the evil redemption, for the weak strength - *I will not return foul for foul, I give only what I have to give, hoodoo blessings,*

8:54:3: when customary life techniques prove inadequate, it is myth and ritual that enable participants to transcend the grind of life and find transcendental meaning in everyday struggle, chanting *de mo ja* expands awareness and brings down da mojo in us all, do not leave the house without your mojo band for emergency stress purposes, dont do nothing without you got your mojo working - ritual, both scheduled and improv, sanctifies life, sanctifies the very grind of it, establishing a connection between the spiritual and the material, seen and unseen worlds,

8:54:4: rickydocs hoodoo holywater, a little rainwater, a dash of florida water, some scent you partial to, some homemade potionwork addressing your current needs - season it on your altar, put a ritual blessing on it and anoint the ear to hear truth, the lips to speak truth, the 3rd eye to see truth, the heart to know it, in the shower or at the sink pour the rest over your head to cleanse the soul and clear the path - the more elaborate the ritualwork the better it work / program but if you feeling rushed just run some tapwater, say some blessings over it, touch a drop to your forehead and you good to go, renewed and refreshed in the struggle of life,

8:54:5: crossroads cleansings are easy, 4 coins at any crossroads will confound your demons & effect a spiritual cleansing, but the best cleansings are ones you ritual up for yourself, consider this basic half moon mantra I just now made up - *when the old moon dies, let the my sins die with it, the new moon will find a new me born* - on the new moon fast, flush, and meditate, perform a good deed or two, contemplate the universe and your place in it, humbly approach the divine, acolyte for a day, every thought / word / deed an act of worship,

8:54:6: cleansed of impurities you start with a fresh slate, I recall the story of a pious woman and a whore who once found themselves in the shadow of god, the whore immediately repent and devote herself to service while the pious woman complain vociferously that the whore polluting her space, so god washed them both clean, the whore of her sins, the pious woman a lifetime of virtue - they will both be allowed to begin anew,

8:54:7: hang a bottle on any tree and it becomes an altar, a doorway between this world and the spiritworld, guardian of your yard, evil spirits / bad vibes attempting to access the premises are distracted by sunlight glinting off the bottles and captured within, the traditional bottletree color is deep blue, a deep cleansing / transcendence, whereas multicolored bottletrees reflect a joyous soul / a celebration of life, some folk do both, folk who want it all - when the wind blows just right you can hear those captured spirits making wild and unruly promises, asking to be freed, but only harmony is allowed in your yard - *no fear will touch me, no anxiety will take root, my soul is untroubled, why should I be afraid,*

live your life in a state of grace
let life itself be holyground,

de mo ja de mo ja de mo ja
de mo ja de mo ja de mo ja

The Hoodoo Book of Flowers

8:55: hoodoo crossroads
old papa joe, sitting at the crossroads, show me the high road, show me the high way

8:55:1: the crossroads is where this world cross the spiritworld, anytime you doing spiritwork you working at the crossroads, where the fabric of reality is thin, where the shape of destiny lies in the choice of the moment and every move changes things, reality work comes easier here, your conjurations are stronger here – destiny binds, legba unbinds,

8:55:2: whenever you find yourself standing at the crossroads, choose wisely, what is the most significant lesson inherent in this moment, where is the mojo - the low road is generally the path of least resistance, it will get you there but you wont necessarily grow from it, you will not be transformed, the high road is the one that the superior personality uses for shaped spiritual growth, the high road is the default of the superior soul,

8:55:3: the crossroads is where Fa will be found, the divine impulse to your greater self, no matter where we are on the hoodoo path we can always do / be better, the highroad is not wedded to any one period / phase / peoples / nothing, there is always a better way, the old you will not make it past this moment, dues must be paid, it is a greater you being born,

8:55:4: the astute rootworker is sensitive to crossroads moments when the shape of the future is in play, the future is an infinite array of possibilities with various %s of potentiality, crossroad points remix the array, setting up new paths to desired realities / futures - ride the board, young conjure, conjure up a future to your liking, one that serves the greater good - in moments like this a ruthless focus on the significant is critical, crossroad points are temporal points that open up certain destinic possibilities while closing down others - *cuidado* - one wrong turn you might not ever find your way home,

8:55:5: did I ever tell you about the time the babajohn met up with old scratch at the crossroads and scratch offer the babajohn whatever he want, so the babajohn asked to be able to see the truth of things and, poof, scratch disappeared,

8:55:6: there is a homeless man walking around downtown memphis in a tattered tophat, a bright blue polyester suit and a satchel of souls in which he keeps signed contracts and $5 dollar bills, if you sign one of his contracts he will give you $5 dollars, you be surprised how many folk sign, souls come cheap in memphis,

8:55:7: some of my favorite mythwork entail a clueless young soldier in vietnam one day realize he is in the middle of history, he had always thought of history as happening to other folk / other times / other places, but vietnam he realize history is always now, that with our every thought / word / deed we write the script of the future, since then he been conscious of himself as historical, wondering what will be wrote when his story is told, forging his legacy, work by work, word by word – *there it is,*

8:55:8: to bring out the best in a situation, apply a liberal application of rickydocs special blend gooberdust, 1st you go to the crossroads and scoop you up a good batch of crossroads dirt, this is your base, add a pinch of graveyard dirt from the graves of loved ones, a little sand from the doorway of no return, a little clutch of dirt from recife, a little dried out mississippi mud from

The Hoodoo Book of Flowers

rickydocs roost, you get the idea, put some glittery stuff in it, stash it on the altar, and you have conjured up you a batch of rickydocs special blend, glittering fairy dust that bring out the magic in any condition, a little sprinkling of rickydocs special blend gooberdust on your path will open the way everytime, your own little portable crossroads, illumination on demand - drop 4 coins for me while you at it - *thankyou* - and remember you cant go buy no helping of rickydocs special blend, got to ritual up your own, cant nobody but you walk this here path,

8:55:9: well that's not totally correct, if you falter call on papa joe, aka, papa gede nibo bey la kwa, geechie lord live out there on rabbit trail road, horse of gullah jack and lord of the crossroads, *in papa joes yard you always protected,* best you take him a crab claw or something oldschool like that, those geechie folk they particular,

embrace de geas of rickydoc and ask me what you will, me and papa joe, we own the crossroads

de mo ja

8:56: hoodoo faith
come katamogun, o keeper of the faith, give me what I need

8:56:1: faith in that which cannot be seen, that which cannot be known, it is faith sustain you when reason fails, when you at the limits of what is known and must take one more step into the abyss, it is faith that allow us to press forward when the way is dim, that allows us to venture beyond the sanctuary of what is known, it is faith assume the universe is ultimately fair,

8:56:2: faith that has not been tested is not faith, strength that has not been tested is not strength, grace that has not been tested is not grace, doubts and anxieties never go away, all you can do is learn to ignore them, have faith in the process, be systematic, leave little to chance, the great mojo does not refuse grace to those who do what they can,

8:56:3: when salif keita joined the rail band in bamako the noble keitas, the line of sundiata keita, disowned him for becoming a nyamakala, a griot, a servant, but he had a Fa that transcended class loyalty, once he became a cultural icon they were quick to reclaim him, sometimes you just gotta leap and figure out how to fly on the way down - *or not* - I recall a keeper of the faith who fell off a cliff and caught a bush on the way down, a voice say have faith, let go of the bush, sister woman did that little head weave and said I need a 2nd opinion, thank you, Ima hold on,

8:56:4: kinda like that well known story from when katrina flooded new orleans, a pious man was caught adrift atop a roof, he prayed to the lord for help but when a boat come by taking folk off nearby roofs he waved it on, the lord will provide, he said, to another boat he told the same thing, and when a helicopter came for the last stragglers it, too, he waved on, confident in the lords provender, and so he died before his time, and when he ascended forthwith to heaven he filed a complaint, lord, he said, I have been faithful to you and yet you let me die without aid, well, say the lord, deeply offended, according to my records here, I sent you two boats and a helicopter,

8:56:5: I respect faith but its doubt that move knowledge, that cause you to question / inquire / judge / evolve - faith and reason must work in hand, blind faith is the faith of a child, blind faith is an illusion, adult faith is hardened faith, seasoned with doubt, to maintain in the face of adversity is a hoodoo act of faith - we have to assume that there is order in this cosmos, gods patterns unseen so much more harmonious than that we see, harmonies far greater than any we sing - when you do lose faith, when you doubt yourself existential, a little shekere work is all it take for katomogun to renew you,

8:56:6: *without faith you are incapable of achieving feats of any magnitude,* a farmer plants a seed in faith of patterns perceived, faith is a witness - there are certain bedrock beliefs I choose not to question, I assume the godhead is essentially benevolent, as are the ancestors and any other spirits I allow into my world - *if you aint benevolent, fuck you* - I choose to see god as a conjuration loop between humanity and divinity - *in faith will I sustain you, I will be with you in troubled times, we will celebrate the good ones and finesse the hard ones, I am the straight lick, the crooked stick, I am shield I am spear and I am willing, be not afraid, let not your soul be troubled, who can undo what I have done, call me I will come,*

8:56:7: *I assume god / the universe does not care about us* one way or the other but that attunement to the laws of nature will prosper one, I assume that god approves of my prophetic practice and, all evidence to the contrary, I assume the gods of literature love me, (apparently they dont want me resting on my laurels so they dont give me none) - I furthermore assume that life is unrelenting struggle blessed with moments of fleeting grace and I have faith that humanity will continue to evolve and grow and meet any challenge the universe throws at us,

I have to believe this in order to go on in the midst of such evident suffering, I believe the spirit is stronger than reality, if I believe it is – de mo ja,

from faith to fruition
is the hoodoo way,

de mo ja

9TH MOVEMENT: IRIE GRACE
gods blessings on us all,

9:57: hoodoo serenity
nanalice marcelene, serenity come

9:57:1: the serene mind is cool, calm and collected in the midst of struggle and the grapple of life, it is a peace of mind that meets adversity with the same serenity you bring to fortune, neither throws you off your game - there is no greater blessing than equanimity, the ability to step back and apply perspective in the blink of the hoodoo eye, something you should practice every day, alert to opportunities to exercise your equanimity, to finesse stress - *come, come, gather up ye mojo,*

9:57:2: happiness is a fleeting emotion tied to the moment, difficult to sustain, happy all the time is unnatural whereas serenity is a default emotion that permeates all others, its expecting to be happy all the time make folk feel lacking when they not, a little melancholy now and then is good for the soul, whatever your condition serenity will improve it, do not waste time or shed mojo on arbitrary worriation,

9:57:3: no such thing as a life without stress, embrace it, use it, an opportunity to once again practice the equanimity that defines you, a walking meditation that transcend the hammer, impervious to the slings of fortune and the daily grind, adept at putting experiences into perspective, a hoodoo traveler are you not, a master of the hoodoo way, a walking meditation programmed in your meditative practice so its available as needed in the grind of life, in the eye of the storm, pride yourself on your equanimity,

The Hoodoo Book of Flowers

9:57:4: the hoodoo adept tends to be an overachiever, got things to do, too much serenity and nothing gets done, it is a serenity of purpose that maintains the players edge, that transcends without losing the focus and the passion, the drive that achieves the unachievable - balance is not stasis, perfect stasis is like death, balance is energies playing against each other in a state of ongoing harmonization, serenity of purpose comes from a certain detachment to the fruits of your labor, no matter how important there has to be a part of you that is removed, at all times the observer. keeping shit in perspective,

9:57:5: attitude is everything, the harshest conditions will not touch the serene soul, but if you are of an agitated spirit and an unsettled mind, nothing will bring you peace -

9:57:6: hoodoo serenity is a core seriousness that which is shallow cannot touch, good or bad serenity accepts it all with equal grace, de bigger de hammer de deeper de cool, a calmness within that generates calmness in everybody in the beam of your radiance, whenever you feel life tearing at your soul ask mama marcelene for a hoodoo gifting - *serenity is your birthright,*

9:57:5: I know everything there is to know, secrets that you had you dont have them no more, love / power / money / even serenity, tell me what you want, I will give you what you need -

come all ye weary, I will give you peace
of mind - de hoodoo gifting of serenity,

de mo ja

The Hoodoo Book of Flowers

9:58: hoodoo mastery
come mama whodun, hoodoo queen,
anoint my soul with mastery

9:58:1: mastery - peak achievement in your chosen field, mastery requires commitment / apprenticeship / study / reflection / engagement, and most of all / obsession, the fruit of training / experience / practice - lo and behold, the pilgrim has gained mastery of self and the disciplined will of a hoodoo traveler, only then can you call yourself a master,

9:58:2: *if you would attempt mastery, young conjure,* you must understand your field of play better than anyone else, you must be a force in it, the consummate professional, through & through, got to love what you do, got to give yourself to it, fully and obsessively, passionately, dues must be paid, you must be religious in your devotion to it, without patience there is no mastery - Im told when coltrane first came out to play they blew him off the stage, Im told old boy went home, went into that woodshed out back and he practice and he practice until he was the john coltrane, came back and said now blow this,

9:58:3: *for 16 years I was part of a cadre of fledglings* that followed the babajohn from school to school, learning what in mystical traditions is called the hidden knowledge - the extended example of the masters life,

9:58:4: *the student without a mentor is a wanderer,* spending years on what should take days, seek out guides who know the road and willing to share, but do remember this, when choosing a hoodoo mentor choose wisely, if it dont seem right likely it aint, never put your fragile little soul in calloused hands, if the student feels any sense of reservation about a prospective mentor might want to look elsewhere - the wrong teacher is worse than no teacher at all,

9:58:5: *a master without students is not a master,* mature mastery entail a certain responsibility to young folk in your tradition, this is a sacred responsibility, leave your ego and your libido at home - do not take on a student who has not made an effort, a student who has come to you on impulse will leave on it, every student taken on is a profound commitment and investiture if done right, dont waste your time or theirs on folk who not serious about this, if the teacher feels any sense of reservation about a student put them to the test - the wrong student is worse than no student at all,

9:58:6: *optimal hoodoo transmission seem to be* folk drawn to your vision, students who hunt you down and insist on being taught, folk who will not be turned away, different versions of your teachings spread by the practical and the visionary, succeeding generations / teachers spread the word, interpret and analyze the teachings, extract from them rules and regulations by which generations live / flower / flourish, gradually form conquers essence, the way fossilizes, another visionary arises to renew and regenerate - *there it is,*

9:58:7: *a master in the field will exude a certain core confidence* that does not need to prove itself, that needs neither acknowledgement nor bluster - in the eternal quest for mastery I suggest you call on mama whodun, closest thing I know to a hoodoo queen, to call down whodun a tarot reading is good but a white candle will suffice, whodun keep it real, a master of the mystical sciences before whom I bow,

o masters of the hoodoo way
dancing on the cutting edge

demoja

9:59: hoodoo transcendent
lady ibeshe, dance me through, take me to higher ground

9:59:1: to transcend, to go beyond your limitations, to evolve beyond where you been, beyond the physical into the spiritual, beyond obstruction, beyond limitation, in human evolution there is always the next step, there is always a way,

9:59:2: the great ways are all instruments of transcendence, preparing you for when divinity manifest in your life and transform you, transcendent moments of awe and wonder, all ways have high and low paths, the path will shape itself to the believer, the truly enlightened can wear any faith like a garment and find its truth,

9:59:3: park yourself at the crossroads to find significance and divine meaning in your daily grind, engage triggers of transcendence that throw you off track and force you into brand new realities, if you a seeker your triggers are often revelation, if you grounded in the physical it takes the hammer - *hoodoo knowledge is knowledge transcendent,*

9:59:4: one day ombure the crocodile god slithered from the great lake and demanded 1 virgin a year *to live with me in the depths of my lake,* many virgins in the villagers defied him and the villagers died and died and died, one night they packed up

The Hoodoo Book of Flowers

and slipped away but ombure cast a great spell - *I am ombure, chief of all the forest, the waters and the storm above, hear the words of my tongue and be quick to act upon my command, hinder those who would flee from me, thwart any plan to deny me* - and so it was the storm hindered them, and the forest confused them, leading them to another side of the very same lake from which ombure slithered and killed and killed and killed - *I am ombure, chief of the waters, chief of the forests, chief of the storm, have my virgin ready when I return* - but this virgin he did not take and 7 months later she delivered a boy who was called son of the crocodile, mistreated & loathed by the village, especially when his mother was taken the very next year and he was left to grow up wild, a fearsome young warrior who had but one friend in the village who cared for him, and when she was chosen for ombures bride the two of them decided to end ombure and his sacrifices once and for all, so all that day he gathered up gourds while she and the women of the village, weary of this annual harvest, brewed pots and pots and pots of palm wine so that when ombure slithered out of the lake he found, instead of his customary virgin trembling in fear, gourds and gourds of palmwine offerings strewn thickly about, and ombure was sorely wroth but a sip of this palmwine intrigued him and dawn found him sprawled drunkenly on the beach and bereft of his power, at which point son of the crocodile raise up he fetish and command lightning - *strike ombure* - but lightning refused, I cannot, said lightning, ombure is my master, and son of the crocodile demanded again - *strike ombure* - I cannot, said lightning, so son of the crocodile stood next to ombure and commanded lightning - *then strike me* - and lightning lit up the beach and all the gourds of palm wine exploded and ombure was no more and the villagers all agree:

there will never again any sacrifice of any living thing, the only sacrifice worth giving is your own,

9:59:5: when I question ATRs sacrificial bloodbath I am told I do not understand the will of the gods - well, I understand god has not asked for all this blood, this just archaic practice that must at some point be left behind, why not now, perhaps we can raise the notion of sacrifice, it is sacrifice for the greater good that ennoble the body politic, it is the generations that benefit from our victories, that pay for our mistakes, the price of power, this hoodoo mission for which we have been born / tempered / ground, the only sacrifice I will accept is your own,

9:59:6: awaken the sleeper, protect the weak, guide the strong the three pillars of hoodoo, both individual - *do what you can when you can* - and destinic - if you live in a democratic society force it to live up to its ideals, an authoritarian society work for its democratization, an affluent society the amelioration of inequity, marginal ones bring them into the polity and level the field - in your life make a contribution to the enhancement of the human condition, hoodoo mission why we are here, if you cant change the world change yourself

9:59:7: the competent high hoodoo is always hoodoo transcendent, as we grow older we decline physically while our spiritual life expands in acceptance of mortality and your impending return to the greater whole, transcendence is always a crossroads, to bring ibeshe down is to rise up transcendent, oddly shaped blue bottles from the bottle tree are her souls delight, rise up children, shake the devil out your soul -

dance, ibeshe, dance,

know me in your heart and
I will know you in mine

de mo ja de mo ja

9:60: hoodoo blessings
bonnies blessings abound

9:60:1: hoodoo blessings are bestowed freely, without thought of credit, worth or recompense, the debt erased, and if necessary, carried - *where there is suffering be its ease, where there is sickness be a healing, be harmony in the chaos, love in the hate, where there is weariness be a resting place, be truth in the midst of illusion* - be the way,

9:60:2: whenever people gather together, strife is unavoidable. dont contribute to it, finesse it, calm it, hoodoo it - the boran, a galla folk, consider tribal peace and harmony a major social goal and *nagya borana*, the peace of the boran, is an all-pervasive understanding that keeps tribal conflict to a minimum, it implies active cooperation and concord, daily prayers and ritual ceremony, when the gadamoji, the illuminated one, cries *pray, pray,* all within hearing desist with de discord and reply nagya, nagya - *peace, peace*.

9:60:3: let us identify daily moments of grace, moments in which you save the world by doing your part, those times when you do not correct an innocent mistake, or take umbrage at a slight, or extract revenge for a wrong, let the impatient cut in, forgo privilege, it is bestowing gratuitous blessings that define a bonded soul, its the small kindnesses that accumulate grace in the world, grace is when you let it slide,

The Hoodoo Book of Flowers

9:60:4: listen, I have a story for you, it is not true, it is merely a story, when the babajohn discovered fire he tried to share his knowledge, traveling the known lands to show different tribes how its done, 4 tribes he visited before the 4th one decided he was a demon and killed him - *years passed* - the first tribe he had visited reserved the power of fire for their priests who became warm and rich while the people froze and starved, the 2nd tribe worshipped the babajohn as a fiery, demanding god who delighted in holywar, the 3rd tribe retained the legend of fire but no longer knew how to make it - *years passed* - by and by the day come the queenmother and 3 acolytes were passing through the 1st tribes territory when one disciple, indignant with anger, preached that it was not right that priests are warm and fed while the people starve and freeze, thats backwards, she said, but the folk she gave fire to betrayed her, the priests took her away and drove the queenmother and her remaining acolytes away, the 2nd tribe a disciple told them the conqueror had been human, only human, a great teacher, perhaps, but certainly not a god to be worshipped, her they burned at the stake, 3rd tribe and before her remaining disciple could speak the queenmother told them, listen, there was once a man discovered fire, this is his story, it is not real, she told them, it is only just a story . . .

9:60:5: in the beginning doondari of the fulani created humanity, when humanity became too proud god created death, when death became too proud god created art - to create harmony out of chaos you must encompass it, radiating bonnies blessings remove suffering from everything in the radiance of your power, in the hands of a good conductor even bad notes contribute to the harmony that is the great mojo,

9:60:6: dzugudini, granddaughter of the monomatapa, had a son with no father, when her own father attempted to punish her

her mother stole his rain charms and taught her daughter how to use them, this power saved her and reunited the warring family under the auspices of mudjadiji, ruler of the day, rain queen of the lovedu and embodiment of the rain goddess, khifidola maru a daja, transformer of clouds and guarantor of seasonal regularity - at the turn of the 21st century, makhobo, 6th of the line, was chosen, and on that day blessings rained down with divine abandon and great abundance,

9:60:7: *do not withhold any good you have to give*, be magnanimous in all things, straight up blessings, let a generosity of spirit define you - *hoodoo them all,*

pray pray
nagya nagya

demoja

9:61: hoodoo grace
my grace in grace ms grace

9:61:1: *I see grace as divine presence in your life,* for some folk grace is gods unearned mercy, for some it is a certain dignity, for some its style, smooth and seamless, not a move wasted, a rightness in the world, all tings irie - I recall a story wherein the priest arrives late to the death bed and is challenged for his tardy grace, what does it matter, he replies, grace is everywhere,

9:61:2: *I assume god the universe is not, as we perceive it, conscious of us*, but I choose to believe that the cosmos is essentially beneficent and rewards evolutionary survival behavior, within that context I too want the confidence that god / the universe will come through for me in times of great need, people have always found god at the limits of their own strength and I too wish to face my troubles with the invincible confidence of gods grace,

9:61:3: - best way to get grace is to give it, divinity in action, godlike, thankful for each and every opportunity to practice grace, to grow in grace, it is the accumulation of small graces that make a better world,

9:61:4: acts of grace can be lifechanging or barely noted, wise advice may not linger but kindness is never forgotten, everybody in life fighting the good fight, backs against the wall, one misstep from going under, a kind word or deed is a hoodoo blessing by the grace of god and the power in you, the generosity of spirit that defines us, acts of kindness exalt both giver and givee,

9:61:5: grace grows in consciousness of grace, in acts of grace that become habits of grace, habits of grace that become a life of grace culminating in a graceful death - grace is how jimmy carter responded when he was diagnosed with cancer, said he has lived a good life and expressed his satisfaction that the carter foundation had helped almost eradicate the guinea worm, *I just want*, he said, *the last guinea worm to die before I do,*

9:61:6: be patient, be steady, grace is what you find when everything else abandon you - *doubts and anxiety have no power in the presence of grace,*

9:61:7: the babajohn was the face of the operation but it was ms grace carried the weight, it was ms grace once told me you

The Hoodoo Book of Flowers

wont find what you want until you can bear what you need, to call down ms grace only good deeds will do, tthe gift of grace: *one act of shameless, unadulterated grace a week, one a day if you are particularly devout, a great heartedness capable of divinity,*

grace is what you find at the crossroads
where your daily grind meet the divine,

shalabongo, shalabongo, o
how grace becomes thee

demoja

9:62: hoodoo Fa
in the name of the conqueror, let this work be done

9:62:1: Fa, a fon word mean fate / destiny / divine narrative / lifelong questing in search of the greater you - *is this the path the gods meant for me, standing at the crossroads what will I be* - Fa is divinity manifesting in human destiny, in the orderly operation of the universe, Fa is finding the path, living the life that will bring the practitioner into conformance with the divinity / Fa itself,

9:62:2: we are all born with a hoodoo mission, a contribution to be made to the common good, finding that mission is your fate / Fa / destiny, it lies in always choosing the highroad - I suspect it is the nature of your suffering, the nature of your particular demons, that determines the shape of your Fa, I believe that our struggles are meaningful, I have to believe that we each of us have a greater destiny, one that we can find and live up to, I believe deviation from Fa is when you deny your destiny,

9:62:3: the queen mother told me she once met a farmer who had found an abandoned eaglet and raised it with his chickens, fullgrown it was still feeding with the chickens, queenmother asked why is this eagle feeding with the chickens, farmer said it thinks it is a chicken, queenmother memphis was not amused, surely not, she said, this is no Fa for an eagle, so she lift the eagle up to the sky and said *fly, eagle,* but the eagle jumped down from her hand and continue feeding with the chickens, so queenmother memphis took that eagle to the highest peak of the highest mountain, held her up and said *fly,* the eagle start to jump down and feed but she look out on the vista of the world laid out before her and like that her wings unfurl and a brand new she eagle launched herself into the wind,

9:62:4: when trying to attune a client to their chosen Fa, make the client conscious of their greater destiny, Fa-track them - *I will make of you a traveler, attuned to the guidance of Fa, making choices that accord with your greater self / your narrative / your vision of who you are / your Fa,*

9:62:5: your best and greatest destiny is not a given, most folk do not live out their best Fa, deviate from Fa and you are not what you could have been, living a life so much less than what the gods intended, this is a tragedy - *you did not listen when Fa spoke, brace yourself* - I suspect we never live out our greatest Fa, a perfect life, who can claim perfection, we are all flawed, all human - *in desperate seach of self / of Fa.*

9:62:6: every morning mawu-lisa gives the Work to legba, who is to live, who is to die, what conditions of life will attend

The Hoodoo Book of Flowers

thee, only legba can change the writing of Fa but it was alaundje, the 1st diviner, who was shown how to write the sacred language of Fa, one that humans can read - I suspect you will find your Fa in service of some sort, if not I have misjudged you,

9:62:7: first time brer rabbit went off planet, it was an accident, he had wandered in looking for some space rations, found a comfortable acceleration couch and settled in for a quick nap, next thing he know they breaking free of the atmosphere, when he is found stowawaying the crew determine they cant carry dead weight, he will have to go out the shuttle port, or maybe they should make a meal of him, tasty rabbit stew be better than those space rations, whilst they debating these unsavory options, brer rabbit access ship programming and download the starmaps into his neurals, then he erase it systemwide, along with all the redundancies and then some, this cause much consternation, but the rabbits position now is that he the only one know the way, I am the master of this game, he claim, and demand forthwith to be made captain of the enterprise, or at least a valued crew member - place assured, he look out on the great canvas of stars and see a universe of possibility - *biggest damn briar patch I ever seen,*

supreme good fortune

demoja

9:63: hoodoo godwork
dear god, in all things, help me be thee

9:63:1: it is I, rickydoc rootdoctor, speak in the name of the old gods - though I figure naming god just us trying to encompass the unencompassable - god / the gods / the force / the cosmos / the universal all / the great mojo - I use them interchangeable according to the poetry of the moment and the nature of the need, my default is *divinity*, witness:

divinity, attend me, *ogotemmeli*, speak to me and I will listen, *grandfather nyikang*, I spread the palms of my hands to thee, *oloddumare transcendent*, thy horse I be, *atai*, just this once and I will never ask again, *chiuta*, bring rain, *mbongo*, bring rain, *thixo of the xhosa*, more rain, *dongo, thundergod of the songhay*, drum thunder, *tsui-goab*, shape shifting thunderer, do not fail me, and you, *most high engai of the maasai*, help me, please, *wuni*, see my path clear – *shalabongo,*

9:63:2: I suspect it matters little to divinity which of the great paths you take, long as it high road you - I doubt god / the universe is conscious of us, yet & still I look for grace, need grace, such need - *shalabongo,*

akongo, bring aid, *nyambe*, bring help, *piercing ala*, pierce illusion, *chuku*, o highest one, *woyengi*, come, *asa of the akamba*, protect me, *modimo*, remove evil from my path, *abassi*, bring joy, *lozi ngewo-wa*, bring blessings, *nyalitch*, in your grace, *ditaolane*, are you there, *kalumba*, are you there, *most high ngai of the kikuyu*, come down from kilimanjaros seat, *enekpe*, listen, *asobe*, wash away my sins, *anna*, let me begin again, *rise domfe*, do not fail me, *o ruwa*, I adore thee, o *meketa of the kono*, I am pure, *almighty asis*, beat the drums, *bilikonda the everlasting eternal one*, judge me worthy, *dear jouk*, I have doubts, *o huveane*, I have questions, *alouroua of the baule*, many questions - *shalabongo,*

The Hoodoo Book of Flowers

9:63:3: gods die / evolve when their believers see the mythwork for what is, when they will no longer live / suffer / die / kill for their god - *early peoples conceived of god as their god, god as tribal mascot* - we know better now and should know no longer be ruled by myths we see through – *shalabongo,*

mbamba kiara, grant us rain, *and you deng,* ancient one of surpassing greatness, do not forsake me, *o imana,* if only you would help me, *khmvoun,* hear our call, mercy for all, *beloved nhialic,* mercy on me, *o yataa,* let blessings abound, *leza,* in your name, *nyame,* the great mantle which covers us all, hear me, *unkulunkulu of the zulu,* come, come, *mwene nyaga,* come, *soko,* come, *kyala,* come when you can, *oyigiyigi,* please come, *ota aiku,* the mighty immovable rock that never dies, come – *shalabongo,*

mawu-lisa, move me, *nhialac,* remove my pain, *tomukujen,* behold my victories, it is well, *lenana,* I pray this day, *dear mother earth,* be gentle with me and I will be gentle in my turn, *o murungu,* we gather in your name, *o rugaba,* accept my offering, *o ruwa,* take my hand, *o epilipili,* hear my plea, for it is you, *nyankonpon,* who alone is great, and what you have made is good, hear my cry, *omari,* let thy wrath cease – *shalabongo,*

9:63:4: me and god got an understanding, I have been given a dispensation that preclude lies and illusions, I have been given a dispensation to break old ways and forge new ones, it was *divinity bid me sing – shalabongo,*

atilo, all praises, *sing qamata,* all praises, *sing mwari,* makongo, sing *nasilele,* makongo, sing *nzame of the bantu, supplier of many cattle, rise up njambi,* are you there, *faro of the bambara,* are you there, *resplendent kwoth,* grant me serenity, *haragakiza,*

The Hoodoo Book of Flowers

every day I pray, *tilo lord*, hear me, *en-kai*, lead me, *tamukujen*, I will not fear if you are with me, *wondrous chieng*, though all stand against me, *almighty asis*, I will not be defeated, *come ankore*, see me, *come mutalabala the eternal*, free me, *come lord ngewo*, deliver me, *and kurumasaba*, sanctify me, *owo*, bless me - *shalabongo*,

9:63:5: *if you believe a thing is so* then you conduct yourself accordingly, if a lot of folk believe it is so then a lot of folk conduct themselves accordingly - *making real into the world that which was not* - be careful therefore what you would conjure into the world, if you would forge a god forge a worthy god - *shalabongo*,

come nana of the akan, who seweth the heavens like kente, *winnamof the mossi,* who dare defy you, *o dearest mungu,* let me be a healing, *o ptah of memphis,* who thought the world, *come down apedemak,* down from jebal barkals peak, *attend me amesami,* we grow in power, *attend me asobe,* I stand before you, *attend me nzambi,* there is sighing & difficulty, *o abuk,* where are you, and *androa of the lugbara,* transcendent beyond knowledge – *shalabongo,*

9:63:6: - *I do not know what god is* but I do know what god is not, no patriarch, no earthmother, no dysfunctional family, no dispenser of virgins - probably presumptuous to think we know all there is to know about god, ongoing revelation by spiritual teachers and scientific discovery - im told folk need god to be somebody you can talk to / beg / cajole / threaten / reward / worship / look to for grace in times of great need / I got no problem communing with the immensity of the great mojo / the godhead - *if anything it is our souls that are in the image of god, not our bodies,*

The Hoodoo Book of Flowers

I have questions, *merciful imana*, I am in distress, *mboko the great mother*, where will I go, what will I do, *kanu dear kanu*, where is there room for me, *ruhanga*, see me, *godfather were*, know me, *kalumba*, grace me, *rugaba*, come, find me, *shilluk*, source of all things, come, *kaang the wonder*, come, *kwoth of the nuer*, god of mystery, *come*, and *mbere*, too and *bantumodimo of the tswana*, rise up, and *mukuru, the old one*, rise up singing, *jah rastafari*

may your days be full of passion, may your lives be full of grace, may your works serve many generations, may gods blessings be on us all,

9:63:7: summer mornings I raise the sun, I take my mbira and I sit on the porch and I listen to the world and I play along with it, and I greet it all with - *hello lord* - the sound of crickets, a jogger, a passing car - *hello lord* - a neighbors cat stepping gingerly through the grass, trees branched against the sky like stained glass in a skydomed cathedral - *hello lord* - to those who listen everything has voice - *hello lord* - peace, compassion, wellbeing, a deeper sense of lifes purpose, moments of divinity and indications of grace, all tings irie - to those who listen anything can be a door to the divine - *hello lord,*

9:63:8: the new york times had a series little while back, humans of new york, a daily photo with quote, random folk in the city, one day they had a picture of a guy in a t-shirt, older guy, your basic new yorker park benching on what is clearly a pretty summer day, who said to interviewer - *god sends me little moments all day long to say, youre not alone, brother, just a little while ago, an old hunched-over chinese lady smiled at me with the greatest warmth in her eyes,*

The Hoodoo Book of Flowers

interviewer: *and you think that was a message from god,*

t-shirt guy: *I think that was god,*

9:63:9: I suspect Im about the slackest holyman ever been, it cross my mind sometime if Im the hope of the race we in bigger trouble than we thought - *who am I to think I could found a Way* - but damn if Ima let history say I had the power but didnt have the heart, I will continue to conduct myself as I aspire to be - *the high hoodoo of memphis* - model of the spiritual & strategic advisors I would the hoodoos of the future be,

most of my understanding comes from failure, I hope in this Work to find a measure of redemption, implanting my destinic vision into the historical record and weaving a message for future generations:

you need me, you call me,
I will come, I am rickydoc,

that is all, this spell is done
demoja demoja demoja

gods blessings on us all

Made in the USA
Columbia, SC
28 January 2025